The Poetry of Lady Mary Wortley Montagu

Lady Mary Wortley Montagu was born on 26th May 1689 to, the soon to be titled, Earl of Kingston and Mary (Fielding) Pierrepoint. At age 3 Mary's mother died and so her Grandmother became responsible for her upbringing in her early years.

Unfortunately, a few years later, when Mary was 9, her grandmother died and so she went back to live with her father at Thoresby Hall, in Nottinghamshire. Women were not formally educated at this time so Mary educated herself in her father's library, teaching herself Latin and devouring many classical texts. She was expected to attend to several of her father's needs however, including presiding over his dinner table where she became a sort of 'good luck charm' for many of his influential guests.

During her teenage years, her true character began to reveal itself. She had already written several volumes of poetry and was intent on challenging social attitudes towards women which stifled their intellectual and social growth.

Defying her father's wishes, she eloped in August 1712, to marry Edward Wortley Montagu. The following year she gave birth to a boy. Unfortunately, her husband, like her father was possessive and jealous. The marriage would not be as successful as she hoped.

Now further tragedy was to strike. Her brother, only 20 years old, contracted and died from smallpox. Mary herself was to catch the disease two years later. Her survival led to her interest in the Turkish procedure of inoculating against the disease by introducing a small amount of the virus in order to build the body's immunity to the disease. She used this method with both of her children and encouraged its' widespread use in London despite resistance and scepticism by British doctors and prevailing medical opinion.

In 1714 Edward Montagu was appointed to the Treasury which allowed Mary to shine at court. Her charm, wit and beauty was appreciated by George I, the Prince of Wales and many other influential and important London figures who soon became friends.

Mary also met the famed poet Alexander Pope who was smitten with her beauty, elegance and wit. Although these feelings were not reciprocated, the two of them did correspond frequently.

Her husband was next appointed as Ambassador to Istanbul (then called Constantinople), for several years. She also gave birth to her daughter, Mary at this time and continued to develop her flamboyant style sporting Turkish inspired clothes which she wore back in the UK contributing further to her distinctive appearance and aristocratic eccentricity.

Her voyage home together with her other travels resulted in her writing sparkling prose in the form of Letters from Turkey. Although at the time many were circulated in manuscript form, as per her wishes, they were not published until a year after her death.

Her letters to Pope were fewer now, although they provide part of the Embassy Letters for which she is so well known. Their subsequent estrangement and enmity now spilled over as each feuded with the other in clever and entertaining poems and publications.

Mary understood that being a woman gave her a unique perspective, allowing her greater access to many places and customs barred to men. As she noted: "You will perhaps be surpriz'd at an Account so different from what you have been entertaind with by the common Voyage-writers who are very fond of speaking of what they don't know".

In 1736, Mary met and fell in love with Francesco Algarotti. By 1739, besotted, she arranged to live with him in Italy, telling her husband and friends she needed to go abroad for her health. Their relationship fell apart in 1741 and Mary would now spend most of her remaining years travelling through Italy and France, putting down roots in several cities.

In 1761, hearing that her husband had died, she returned home to England. She arrived in London in January 1762. It was to be her final journey.

Lady Mary Wortley Montagu died on 21st August 1762 in London.

Index of Contents

Introduction

Lady Mary Wortley Montagu was born in 1689 in London; her father was Evelyn Pierrepont, Earl of Kingston, a Yorkshire gentleman. She was the eldest child. Her mother, Lady Mary Fielding, died after bearing her fourth child, when Mary was still quite young. The Earl enjoyed the company of women and was not much inclined to take an interest in the children. After they were grown and out of the house he married a woman younger than any of them.

The children were raised by their paternal grandmother in Yorkshire. At a very early age Mary took over her mother's duties in presiding at the Earl's table. This meant that she must carve the meat for all the guests, who were often numerous. This was arduous and she learned to have dinner early so she could concentrate on her work to her fathers' satisfaction.

Young Mary was always fascinated by literature. Determining to learn to read Ovid in the original, she took a Latin grammar and dictionary from the family library and hid with them for several hours a day for two years. She thus became competent in Latin and her father, upon discovering this, was pleased enough to have her tutored in Italian; she also learned French, and, years later, Turkish.

Her own collection of books, later in life, consisted mostly of English drama, as far back as Gammer Gurton's Needle. She also particularly enjoyed novels, such as those of Fielding, who was her cousin, and whose work she helped establish.

It was Mary's ability to quote Horace in the original that attracted the attention of Edward Wortley Montagu, who believed, unlike many others, that women should be literate and educated. Montagu had gone to Cambridge, then the Middle Temple, and was called to the bar in 1699. He traveled on the Continent in 1701-3, with Joseph Addison, a close friend. From 1705 on, Wortley Montagu spent most of his life in Parliament and was a noted speaker in the Whig cause.

Wortley Montagu corresponded with Mary for seven years before he really concluded to marry her in 1712. In the meantime, her father decided to marry her to a boorish lord who could offer more money than Montagu, and shipped her off to marry him. She determined to elope and had Wortley follow her coach and steal her from an inn in the middle of the night.

Wortley admired his wife's intellect and offered her services as a critic to Addison on his tragedy, Cato. She was shy about this and told Addison she was only doing it on the orders of her husband. Her essay praises Addison's characterization but savages his plot, and makes many pointed suggestions. He actually followed most of them, but asked that her essay never see the light of day. It was not published until this century.

In 1713 Lady Mary's first child, Edward Wortley Montagu, was born. She doted on him when he was small and worked hard at parenting, but he proved to be completely incorrigible. Edward periodically ran away from home, and eventually was placed on the Continent with a tutor who had to watch him night and day. If he escaped he forged his parents' signatures and ran up huge debts. He married several women, not all at the same time, but never bothered with divorce.

In 1714 Lady Mary wrote a Spectator, #573, for Addison, in the guise of a letter from Mrs. President of a club of widows. She describes her six dead husbands as worthless fellows who none of them rated a very long mourning. It is powerful feminist satire and a very good novella packed into four pages.

In that year, Queen Anne died and Wortley Montague's fortunes improved. He was a Lord of the Treasury under George I. It became possible for Lady Mary, who had been kept mostly in the country, to move to London. She was an instant hit in society and became a friend of Gay and Pope. Gay was at this time inventing a genre called Town Eclogue, adapting pastoral conventions to London doings, and had a half-finished example by him. He and Lady Mary completed differing versions of it, and she set out producing a whole set of them, one for each day except Sunday. These were much admired, and two of them, along with the one written with Gay, found their way into print. Curll, the publisher, had done this without permission, and Pope invited him to tea and administered an emetic in revenge, then published a poem detailing the effects. Lady Mary was not named in the volume, but was hinted at, and became known as something of a literary figure. Pope laboriously copied out the five that were Lady Mary's into a handsomely bound blank-book, which rests today in the New York Public Library.

In 1716 Wortley Montagu was appointed ambassador to Turkey. His family's long and dangerous journey over the Continent in dead of winter was considered something of an achievement at the time. Lady Mary enjoyed it all, and kept up a constant correspondence with friends in England, writing in a style that eventually established her permanent epistolary reputation. Constantinople was full of wonders which Lady Mary, unlike so many European wives, set out to explore and understand. She mastered the language, investigated mosques, and visited with the women of the harem, whom she came to admire. She discovered that the Turks inoculated for smallpox, and determined to bring the practice to England.

Alexander Pope corresponded with her during this time, and sent her a copy of his "Eloise to Abelard," and she finding a line from one of her Town Eclogues in it, wrote in the margin: mine!

Wortley was recalled due to a change in English relations with Turkey, and the family, with a new daughter (later the Countess of Bute), appeared in London in the fall of 1718. Pope had Lady Mary's picture painted by Godfrey Kneller, wrote some verses on it which are still printed in his works, and it hung in his best room for the rest of his life. The Wortley Montagus settled in his neighborhood at Twickenham, and he is said to have made an effort to declare his love openly to her in about the year 1722. She tried unsuccessfully to stifle an amused laugh, upon which he became her enemy forever after.

At the same time Lady Mary was struggling to interest the English medical establishment in inoculation. Their main objection seems to have been to being told by a woman what it was their business to know. She did succeed in defeating smallpox in England, but barely succeeded in being thanked for it, and her relations with high society worsened steadily, especially when Pope began attacking her honor (on the point of chastity) in verse.

Lady Mary became a great friend of Lord Hervey, who was satirized by Pope as Lord Fanny. She herself said the world was made up of "men, women, and Herveys." She worked closely with Hervey in composing replies to Pope, and in these poems are found some of her best lines. But it was like pouring oil on the flames. Anything Pope wrote was going to be read everywhere and for decades, if not centuries, and Lady Mary was helping to create a situation which endangered the career and social standing of her husband, a member of Parliament.

In 1737 she took a hand in helping her husband's party by bringing out, anonymously, a newspaper against the popular Opposition paper Common-Sense. Hers was called The Nonsense of Common-sense. It ran for at least nine numbers.

"Lewis Gibbs" (pseud., writing in 1949) suggests that, as Pope's malevolence continued unabated and included Wortley (as a cuckold and a dull miser), it was determined in family council that Lady Mary should go into exile and not return until after his death. Robert Halsband, who had access to more correspondence than Gibbs or anyone previously, says that, just as was rumored at the time Lady Mary actually had hopes of joining a lover, the handsome young Italian author Algarotti. Lord Hervey was also infatuated with Algarotti, and the two appear to have competed for his attention; neither in the end was successful. Lady Mary, who was forty-seven at this time, did go to the continent, did not manage to settle down with Algarotti or any other lover that we know of, and lived in France and Italy for twenty years without seeing her husband in all this time. He gave her a generous allowance and corresponded with her, especially about their troublesome son, and kept all her letters. He asked her to see Naples and describe it to him. He lived into his eighties, and shortly after his death Lady Mary returned to London, already dying of breast cancer. She died in August 1762, age 73.

Lady Mary's daughter had meanwhile married Lord Bute, who became George III's right hand man. It was important to Mary, Countess of Bute, to maintain the utmost propriety in eyes of the world, and the most probable source of any possible embarrassment was her mother. Lady Mary wrote a history of her times, and this could have made trouble, but as she assured her daughter, each chapter was destroyed as soon as it was written. Lady Mary had also kept a journal all her life; this the Countess came into possession of, and kept it long suppressed, and then burned it. Only a short memoir of the court of George I survives of these materials; it is considered a valuable document by historians, and is a vivid example of Lady Mary's excellent prose.

When Lady Mary was about to return for the last time to England, she asked Rev. Sowden to keep for publication her Embassy Letters. When her family heard of this manuscript they offered five hundred pounds for it, and got it, but to their horror another copy had been made, and the work was published. It was an overnight sensation, and went into multiple editions. Dr. Samuel Johnson loved the letters, and Edward Gibbon said of them, "What fire, what ease, what knowledge of Europe and Asia." Lady Mary had triumphed over the strictures of a society in which publishing one's work was unseemly for a woman, especially one of high rank, and over the objections and stratagems of a family that subscribed to these strictures. She had secured perhaps the only thing she really ever wanted: lasting, and deserved, literary fame.

PROSE

ACCOUNT OF THE COURT OF GEORGE THE FIRST AT HIS ACCESSION

I Was then in Yorkshire; Mr. W. (who had, at that time, that sort of passion for me, that would have made me invisible to all but himself, had it been in his power) had sent me thither. He stayed in town on the account of some business, and the Queen's death detained him there. Lord Halifax, his near relation, was put at the head of the Treasury; and, willing to have the rest of the commissioners such as he thought he could depend on, named him for one of them. It will be surprising to add that he hesitated to accept of it, at a time when his father was alive and his present income very small; but he had that opinion of his own merit as made him think any offer below that of Secretary of State not worth his acceptance, and had certainly refused it if he had not been persuaded to the contrary by a rich old uncle of mine, Lord Pierrepont, whose fondness for me gave him expectations of a large legacy.

The new court with all their train was arrived before I left the country. The Duke of Marlborough was returned in a sort of triumph, with the apparent merit of having suffered for his fidelity to the succession, and was reinstated in his office of General, &c. In short, all people who had suffered any hardship or disgrace during the late ministry, would have it believed that it was occasioned by their attachment to the House of Hanover. Even Mr. Walpole, who had been sent to the Tower for a piece of bribery proved upon him, was called a confessor to the cause. But he had another piece of good luck that yet more contributed to his advancement; he had a very handsome sister, whose folly had lost her reputation in London; but the yet greater folly of Lord Townshend, who happened to be a neighbor in

Norfolk to Mr. Walpole, had occasioned his being drawn in to marry her some months before the Queen died.

Lord Townshend had that sort of understanding which commonly makes men honest in the first part of their lives; they follow the instruction of their tutor, and, till somebody thinks it worth their while to show them a new path, go regularly on in the road where they are set. Lord Townshend had then been many years an excellent husband to a sober wife, a kind master to all his servants and dependents, a serviceable relation wherever it was in his power, and followed the instinct of nature in being fond of his children. Such a sort of behaviour without any glaring absurdity, either in prodigality or avarice, always gains a man the reputation of being reasonable and honest; and this was his character when the Earl of Godolphin sent him envoy to the States, not doubting but he would be faithful to his orders, without giving himself the trouble of criticising on them, which is what all ministers wish in an envoy. Robotun, a French refugee (secretary to Bernstoff, one of the Elector of Hanover's ministers), happened to be at the Hague, and was civilly received at Lord Townshend's, who treated him at his table with the English hospitality, and he was charmed with a reception which his birth and education did not entitle him to. Lord Townshend was recalled when the Queen changed her ministry; his wife died, and he retired into the country, where (as I have said before) Walpole had art enough to make him marry his sister Dolly. At that time, I believe, he did not propose much more advantage by the match than to get rid of a girl that lay heavy on his hands.

When King George ascended the throne, he was surrounded by all his German ministers and playfellows male and female. Baron Goritz was the most considerable among them both for birth and fortune. He had managed the King's treasury thirty years with the utmost fidelity and economy; and had the true German honesty, being a plain, sincere, and unambitious man. Bernstoff the secretary was of a different turn. He was avaricious, artful, and designing; and had got his share in the King's councils by bribing his women. Robotun was employed in these matters, and had the sanguine ambition of a Frenchman. He resolved there should be an English ministry of his choosing; and knowing none of them personally but Townshend, he had not failed to recommend him to his master, and his master to the King, as the only proper person for the important post of Secretary of State; and he entered upon that office with universal applause, having at that time a very popular character, which he might possibly have retained for ever if he had not been entirely governed by his wife and her brother R. Walpole, whom he immediately advanced to be Paymaster, esteemed to be a post of exceeding profit, and very necessary for his indebted estate.

But he had yet higher views, or rather he found it necessary to move higher, lest he should not be able to keep that. The Earl of Wharton, now Marquis, both hated and despised him. His large estate, the whole income of which was spent in the service of the party, and his own parts, made him considerable; though his profligate life lessened the weight that a more regular conduct would have given him.

Lord Halifax, who was now advanced to the dignity of Earl, graced with the Garter, and First Commissioner of the Treasury, treated him with contempt. The Earl of Nottingham, who had the real merit of having renounced the ministry in Queen Anne's reign, when he thought they were going to alter the succession, was not to be reconciled to Walpole, whom he looked upon as stigmatised for corruption. The Duke of Marlborough, who in his old age was making almost the same figure at court that he did when he first came into it—I mean, bowing and smiling in the ante-chamber, while Townshend was in the closet—was not, however, pleased with Walpole, who began to behave to him with the insolence of new favour; and his Duchess, who never restrained her tongue in her life, used to make public jokes of the beggary she first knew him in, when her caprice gave him a considerable place, against the opinion of Lord Godolphin and the Duke of Marlborough.

To balance these, he had introduced some friends of his own, by his recommendation to Lord Townshend (who did nothing but by his instigation). Colonel Stanhope was made the other Secretary of State. He had been unfortunate in Spain, and there did not want those who attributed it to ill conduct; but he was called generous, brave, true to his friends, and had an air of probity that prejudiced the world in his favour.

The King's character may be comprised in very few words. In private life he would have been called an honest blockhead; and Fortune, that made him a king, added nothing to his happiness, only prejudiced his honesty, and shortened his days. No man was ever more free from ambition; he loved money, but loved to keep his own, without being rapacious of other men's. He would have grown rich by saving, but was incapable of laying schemes for getting; he was more properly dull than lazy, and would have been so well contented to have remained in his little town of Hanover, that if the ambition of those about him had not been greater than his own, we should never have seen him in England: and the natural honesty of his temper, joined with the narrow notions of a low education, made him look upon his acceptance of the crown as an act of usurpation, which was always uneasy to him. But he was carried by the stream of the people about him, in that, as in every other action of his life. He could speak no English, and was past the age of learning it. Our customs and laws were all mysteries to him, which he neither tried to understand, nor was capable of understanding if he had endeavoured it. He was passively good-natured, and wished all mankind enjoyed quiet, if they would let him do so. The mistress that followed him hither was so much of his own temper, that I do not wonder at the engagement between them. She was duller than himself, and consequently did not find out that he was so, and had lived in that figure at Hanover almost forty years (for she came hither at threescore), without meddling in any affairs of the electorate; content with the small pension he allowed her, and the honour of his visits when he had nothing else to do, which happened very often. She even refused coming hither at first, fearing that the people of England, who, she thought, were accustomed to use their kings barbarously, might chop off his head in the first fortnight; and had not love or gratitude enough to venture being involved in his ruin. And the poor man was in peril of coming hither without knowing where to pass his evenings; which he was accustomed to do in the apartments of women, free from business. But Madame Kilmansegg saved him from this misfortune. She was told that Mademoiselle Schulemberg scrupled this terrible journey; and took that opportunity of offering her service to his Majesty, who willingly accepted of it, though he did not offer to facilitate it to her by the payment of her debts, which made it very difficult for her to leave Hanover without the permission of her creditors. But she was a woman of wit and spirit, and knew very well of what importance this step was to her fortune. She got out of town in a disguise, and made the best of her way in a post-chaise to Holland, from which she embarked with the King, and arrived at the same time with him in England; which was enough to make her called his mistress; or at least so great a favourite that the whole court began to pay her uncommon respect.

This lady deserves I should be a little particular in her character, there being something in it worth speaking of. She was past forty: she had never been a beauty, but certainly very agreeable in her person when adorned by youth; and had once appeared so charming to the King, that it was said the divorce and ruin of his beautiful Princess, the Duke of Zell's daughter, was owing to the hopes her mother (who was declared mistress to the King's father, and all-powerful in his court) had of setting her daughter in her place; and that the project did not succeed, by the passion that Madame Kilmansegg took for M. Kilmansegg, who was son of a merchant of Hamburg, and, after having a child by him, there was nothing left for her but to marry him. Her ambitious mother ran mad with the disappointment, and died in that deplorable manner, leaving 40,000 [pounds], which she had heaped by the favour of the Elector, to this daughter, which was very easily squandered by one of her temper. She was both luxurious and generous, devoted to her pleasures, and seemed to have taken Lord Rochester's resolution of avoiding all sorts of self-denial. She had a greater vivacity in conversation than ever I knew in a German of either sex. She loved reading, and had a taste of all polite learning. Her humour was easy and sociable. She was well bred and amusing in company. She knew how both to please and be pleased, and had experience enough to know it was hard to do either without money. Her unlimited expenses had left her very little remaining, and she made what haste she could to make advantages of the opinion the English had of her power with the King, by receiving the presents that were made her from all quarters, and which she knew very well must cease when it was known that the King's idleness carried him to her lodgings without either regard for her advice, or affection for her person, which time and very bad paint had left without any of the charms that had once attracted him. His best- beloved mistress remained still at Hanover, which was the beautiful Countess of Platen.

Perhaps it will be thought a digression in this place to tell the story of his amour with her; but, as I write only for myself, I shall always think I am at liberty to make what digressions I think fit, proper or improper; besides that in my opinion nothing can set the King's character in a clearer light. That lady was married to Madame Kilmansegg's brother, the most considerable man in Hanover for birth and fortune; and her beauty was as far beyond that of any of the other women that appeared. However, the King saw her every day without taking notice of it, and contented himself with his habitual commerce with Mademoiselle Schulemberg.

In those little courts there is no distinction of much value but what arises from the favour of the Prince, and Madame Platen saw with great indignation that all her charms were passed over unregarded, and she took a method to get over this misfortune which would never have entered into the head of a woman of sense, and yet which met with wonderful success. She asked an audience of his Highness, who granted it without guessing what she meant by it; and she told him that as nobody could refuse her the first rank in that place, it was very mortifying to see his Highness not show her any mark of favour; and as no person could be more attached to his person than herself, she begged with tears in her fine eyes that he would alter his behaviour to her. The Elector, very much astonished at this complaint, answered that he did not know any reason he had given her to believe he was wanting in his respect for her, and that he thought her not only the greatest lady, but the greatest beauty of the court. "If that be true, sire," replied she, sobbing, "why do you pass all your time with Schulemberg, while I hardly receive the honour of a visit from you?" His Highness promised to mend his manners, and from that time was very assiduous in waiting on her. This ended in a fondness, which her husband disliked so much that he parted with her; and she had the glory of possessing the heart and person of her master, and to turn the whole stream of courtiers that used to attend Mademoiselle Schulemberg to her side. However, he did not break with his first love, and often went to her apartment to cut paper, which was his chief employment there; which the Countess of Platen easily permitted him, having often occasion for his absence. She was naturally gallant, and, after having thus satisfied her ambition, pursued her warmer inclinations.

Young Craggs came about this time to Hanover, where his father sent him to take a view of that court in his tour of travelling. He was in his first bloom of youth and vigour, and had had so strong an appearance of that perfection, that it was called beauty by the generality of women: though, in my opinion, there was a coarseness in his face and shape that had more the air of a porter than a gentleman, and if Fortune had not interposed her almighty power, he might, by his birth, have appeared in that figure, his father being nothing more considerable at his first appearance in the world than footman to Lady Mary

Mordant, the gallant Duchess of Norfolk, who had always half a dozen intrigues to manage. Some servant must always be trusted in affairs of that kind, and James Craggs had the good fortune to be chosen for that purpose. She found him both faithful and discreet, and he was soon advanced to the dignity of valet-de-chambre.

King James II. had an amour with her after he was upon the throne, and respected the Queen enough to endeavour to keep it entirely from her knowledge. James Craggs was the messenger between the King and the Duchess, and did not fail to make the best use of so important a trust. He scraped a great deal of money from the bounty of this royal lover, and was too inconsiderable to be hurt by his ruin; nor did not concern himself much for that of his mistress, which by lower intrigues happened soon after. This fellow, from the report of all parties, and even from that of his professed enemies, had a very uncommon genius; a head well turned for calculation; great industry; and was so just an observer of the world, that the meanness of his education never appeared in his conversation. The Duke of Marlborough, who was sensible how well he was qualified for affairs that required secrecy, employed him as his procurer both for women and money; and he acquitted himself so well of these trusts as to please his master, and yet raise a considerable fortune, by turning his money in the public funds, the secret of which came often to his knowledge by the Duke's employing him. He had this only son, whom he looked on with the partiality of a parent; and resolved to spare nothing in his education that could add to his figure.

Young Craggs had a great vivacity, a happy memory, and flowing elocution; he was brave and generous; and had an appearance of open- heartedness in his manner that gained him a universal good-will, if not a universal esteem. It is true, there appeared a heat and want of judgment in all his words and actions, which did not make him very valuable in the eyes of cool judges, but Madame Platen was not of that number. His youth and fire made him appear a conquest worthy her charms, and her charms made her appear very well worthy his passionate addresses. Two people so well disposed towards one another were very soon in the closest engagement; and the first proof Madame Platen gave him of her affection was introducing him to the favour of the Elector, who took it on her word that he was a young man of extraordinary merit, and he named him for Cofferer at his first accession to the crown of England, and I believe it was the only place that he then disposed of from any inclination of his own. This proof of Madame Platen's power hindered her coming hither. Bernstoff was afraid she might meddle in the disposition of places that he was willing to keep in his own hands; and he represented to the King that the Roman Catholic religion that she professed was an insuperable bar to her appearance in the court of England, at least so early; but her gave her private hopes that things might be so managed as to make her admittance easy when the King was settled in his new dominions. And with this hope she consented without much concern to let him go without her; not reflecting that weak minds lose all impressions by even short absences. But as her own understanding did not furnish her with very great refinements, she was troubled with none of the fears that would have affected a stronger head, and had too good an opinion of her own beauty to believe anything in England could efface it; while Madame Kilmansegg attached herself to the one thing necessary,— getting what money she could by the sale of place, and the credulity of those who thought themselves very politic in securing her favour.

Lord Halifax was one of this number; his ambition was unbounded, and he aimed at no less than the Treasurer's staff, and thought himself in a fine road to it by furnishing Madame Kilmansegg both with money and a lover. Mr. Methuen was the man he picked out for that very purpose. He was one of the Lords of the Treasury; he was handsome and well- made; he had wit enough to be able to affect any part he pleased, and a romantic turn in his conversation that could entertain a lady with as many adventures as Othello,—and it is no ill way of gaining Desdemonas. Women are very apt to take their lovers' characters from their own mouths; and if you will believe Mr. Methuen's account of himself, neither Artamenes nor Oroondates ever had more valour, honour, constancy, and discretion. Half of these bright qualities were enough to charm Madame Kilmansegg; and they were very soon in the strictest familiarity, which continued for different reasons, to the pleasure of both parties, till the arrival of Mademoiselle Schulemberg, which was hastened by the German ministers, who envied the money accumulated by Madame Kilmansegg, which they had longed to turn into another channel; which they thought would be more easily drawn into their own hands. They took care to inform Mademoiselle Schulemberg of the fond reception all the Germans met in England, and gave her a view of the immense fortune that waited for her here. This was enough to cure her fears, and she arrived accompanied with a young niece who had already made some noise at Hanover. She had projected the conquest of the Prince of Wales, and had so far succeeded as to obtain his favours for some few months; but the Princess, who dreaded a rival to her power, soon put an end to the correspondence, and she was no longer possessed of his good graces when he came hither.

I have not yet given the character of the Prince. The fire of his temper appeared in every look and gesture; which, being unhappily under the direction of a small understanding, was every day throwing him upon some indiscretion. He was naturally sincere, and his pride told him that he was placed above constraint; not reflecting that a high rank carries along with it a necessity of a more decent and regular behaviour than is expected from those who are not set in so conspicuous a light. He was so far from being of that opinion, that he looked on all the men and women he saw as creatures he might kick or kiss for his diversion; and whenever he met with any opposition in those designs, he thought his opposers impudent rebels to the will of God, who created them for his use, and judged of the merit of all people by their ready submission to his orders, or the relation they had to his person. And in this view he looked upon the Princess as the most meritorious of her sex; and she took care to keep him in that sentiment by all the arts she was mistress of. He had married her by inclination; his good-natured father had been so complaisant to let him choose a wife for himself. She was of the house of Anspach, and brought him no great addition either of money or alliance; but was at that time esteemed a German beauty, and had that genius which qualified her for the government of a fool, and made her despicable in the eyes of all men of sense; I mean a low cunning, which gave her an inclination to cheat all the people she conversed with, and often cheated herself in the first place, by showing her the wrong side of her interest, not having understanding enough to observe that falsehood in conversation, like red on the face, should be used very seldom and very sparingly, or they destroy that interest and beauty they are designed to heighten.

Her first thought on her marriage was to secure to herself the sole and whole direction of her spouse; and to that purpose counterfeited the most extravagant fondness for his person; yet, at the same time, so devoted to his pleasures (which she often told him were the rule of all her thoughts and actions), that whenever he thought proper to find them with other women, she even loved whoever was instrumental to his entertainment, and never resented anything but what appeared to her a want of respect for him; and in this light she really could not help taking notice that the presents made to her on her wedding were not worthy of his bride, and at least she ought to have had all his mother's jewels. This was enough to make him lose all respect to his indulgent father. He downright abused his ministers, and talked impertinently to his old grandmother the Princess Sophia; which ended in such a coldness towards all his family as left him entirely under the government of his wife.

The indolent Elector contented himself with showing his resentment by his silence towards him; and this was the situation the family first appeared in when they came into England. This behaviour did not, however, hinder schemes being laid by various persons of gratifying their ambition, or making their fortune, by particular attachments to each of the royal family.

A LETTER FROM THE OTHER WORLD, TO A LADY, FROM HER FORMER HUSBAND

This letter will surprise you less than it would any other of your sex, and therefore I think I need no apology in breaking through a rule of good-breeding, which has been observed so strictly by all husbands for so many ages; who, however troublesome while they lived, have never frightened their wives by the least notice of them after their deaths: but your reverend doctor will inform you, that there is nothing supernatural in this correspondence; and that the existence of immortal spirits includes a tender concern for the poor militant mortals of your world. I own I was a little puzzled how to convey this epistle, and thought it best to assume a material form some moments, and put it myself into the penny-post. In my hurry (being very impatient to let you hear from me) I unluckily forgot my little finger, which produced an odd accident; for the wench at the post-office would have taken me up for one of the incendiaries. Already had the mob assembled round the door, and nothing but dissolving into air could have saved me from Newgate. Several ran down the alleys in pursuit of me; and particular care was taken of my letter, in hopes of reading it in the newspaper. You may imagine I would not have exposed myself to this adventure, but out of the sincerest regard to the happiness of the dear partner of my worldly cares. Without the least uneasiness I have seen you dispose of yourself into the arms of another; and I would never disturb you while you were seeking pleasure in forgetting me; but I cannot bear that you should constrain yourself out of respect to me. I see every motion of your mind now much clearer than I did in my life (though then I guessed pretty shrewdly sometimes). I know the real content that you find in coloured riband, and am sensible how much you sacrifice to imaginary decency every time you put on that odious rusty black, which is half worn out. Alas! my dear Eliza, in these seats of perfect love and beauty, the veriest scrub of a cherubim (some of which have raked cinders behind Montagu House, as they often tell me) is more charming than you were on your first wedding-day. Judge, then, whether I can have any satisfaction in looking at your crape hood when I am in this bright company. You know that, in my terrestrial state, three bottles would sometimes raise me to that pitch of philosophy, I utterly forgot you, when you were but some few inches from me. Do not fancy me grown so impertinent here, as to observe so nicely whether you obey the forms of widowhood; and do not think to cajole me with such instances of your affection, when you are giving the most substantial proofs of it to another man. I have already assured you I am exalted above jealousy, if I could have been sensible of it. You have provoked me by a second choice, so absolutely opposite to your first. He is often talking of certain fellows he calls Classic Authors, who I never trouble my head with: and I know this letter will meet with more regard from him than from you; for he is better skilled in the language of the dead than the living.

IN A PAPER CALLED THE NONSENSE OF COMMON SENSE

Published January 24, 1738

I have always, as I have already declared, professed myself a friend, though I do not aspire to the character of an admirer, of the fair sex; and as such, I am warmed with indignation at the barbarous treatment they have received from the Common Sense of January 14, and the false advice that he gives them. He either knows them very little, or, like an interested quack, prescribes such medicines as are likely to hurt their constitutions. It is very plain to me, from the extreme partiality with which he speaks of Operas, and the rage with which he attacks both Tragedy and Comedy, that the author is a Performer in the Opera; and whoever reads his paper with attention, will be of my opinion; else no thing alive would assert, at the same time, the innocence of an entertainment, contrived wholly to soften the mind and sooth the sense, without any pretence to a moral; and so vehemently declaim against plays, whose end is, to show the fatal consequences of vice, to warn the innocent against the snares of a well-bred designing Dorimant. You see there to what insults a woman of wit, beauty, and quality, is exposed, that has been seduced by the artificial tenderness of a vain agreeable gallant; and, I believe, that very comedy has given more checks to ladies in pursuit of present pleasures, so closely attended with shame and sorrow, than all the sermons they have ever heard in their lives. But this author does not seem to think it possible to stop their propensity to gallantry by reason or reflection. He only desires them to fill up their time with all sorts of trifles: in short, he recommends to them gossiping, scandal, lying, and a whole troop of follies, instead of it, as the only preservatives for their virtue.

I am for treating them with more dignity; and, as I profess myself a protector of all the oppressed, I shall look upon them as my peculiar care. I expect to be told this is downright Quixotism, and that I am venturing to engage the strongest part of mankind, with a paper helmet upon my head. I confess it is an undertaking where I cannot foresee any considerable success; and, according to an author I have read somewhere,

"The world will still be ruled by knaves
And fools, contending to be slaves."

But, however, I keep up the character of a moralist, and shall use my endeavours to relieve the distressed, and defeat vulgar prejudices, whatever the event may be. Among the most universal errors, I reckon that of treating the weaker sex with a contempt which has a very bad influence on their conduct. How many of them think it excuse enough to say they are women, to indulge any folly that comes into their heads! This renders them useless members of the commonwealth, and only burdensome to their own families, where the wise husband thinks he lessens the opinion of his own understanding, if he at any time condescends to consult his wife's. Thus, what reason nature has given them is thrown away, and a blind obedience expected from them by all their ill-natured masters; and, on the other side, as blind a complaisance shown by those that are indulgent, who say often, that women's weakness must be complied with, and it is a vain troublesome attempt to make them hear reason.

I attribute a great part of this way of thinking, which is hardly ever controverted, either to the ignorance of authors, who are many of them heavy collegians, that have never been admitted to politer conversations than those of their bed-makers, or to the design of selling their works, which is generally the only view of writing, without any regard to truth, or the ill consequences that attend the propagation of wrong notions. A paper smartly wrote, though perhaps only some old conceits dressed in new words, either in rhyme or prose—I say rhyme, for I have seen no verses wrote for many years— such a paper, either to ridicule or declaim against the ladies, is very welcome to the coffee-houses, where there is hardly one man in ten but fancies he has some reason or other to curse some of the sex most heartily. Perhaps his sister's fortunes are to run away with the money that would be better bestowed at the Groom-porter's; or an old mother, good for nothing, keeps a jointure from a hopeful son, that wants to make a settlement on his mistress; or a handsome young fellow is plagued with a wife, that will remain alive, to hinder his running away with a great fortune, having two or three of them in love with him. These are serious misfortunes, that are sufficient to exasperate the mildest tempers to a contempt of the sex: not to speak of lesser inconveniences, which are very provoking at the time they are felt.

How many pretty gentlemen have been unmercifully jilted by pert hussies, after having curtseyed to them at half a dozen operas; nay, permitted themselves to be led out twice; yet, after these encouragements, which amount very near to an engagement, have refused their billets-doux, and perhaps married other men, under their noses. How welcome is a couplet or two, in scorn of woman-kind, to such a disappointed lover; and with what comfort he reads, in many profound authors, that they are never to be pleased but by coxcombs; and, consequently, he owes his ill success to the brightness of his understanding, which is beyond female comprehension. The country squire is confirmed, in the elegant choice he has made, in preferring the conversation of his hounds to that of his wife; and the kind keepers, a numerous sect, find themselves justified in throwing away their time and estates on a parcel of jilts, when they read that neither birth nor education can make any of the sex rational creatures; and they can have no value, but what is to be seen in their faces.

Hence springs the applause with which such libels are read; but I would ask the applauders, if these notions, in their own nature, are likely to produce any good effect towards reforming the vicious, instructing the weak, or guiding the young? I would not every day tell my footman, if I kept any, that their whole fraternity were a pack of scoundrels; that lying and stealing were inseparable qualities from their cloth; that I should think myself very happy in them, if they would confine themselves to innocent lies, and would only steal candles' ends. On the contrary, I would say in their presence, that birth and money were accidents of fortune, that no man was to be seriously despised for wanting them; that an honest faithful servant was a character of more value than an insolent corrupt lord; that the real distinction between man and man lay in his integrity, which, in one shape or other, generally met with its reward in the world, and could not fail of giving the highest pleasure, by a consciousness of virtue, which every man feels that is so happy to possess it.

With this gentleness would I treat my inferiors, with much greater esteem would I speak to that beautiful half of mankind who are distinguished by petticoats. If I were a divine, I would remember, that in their first creation they were designed as a help for the other sex; and nothing was ever made incapable of the end of its creation. 'Tis true, the first lady had so little experience that she hearkened to the persuasion of an impertinent dangler; and if you mind, he succeeded, by persuading her she was not so wise as she should be.

Men that have not sense enough to show any superiority in their arguments, hope to be yielded to by a faith, that as they are men, all the reason that has been allotted to human-kind has fallen to their share. I am seriously of another opinion. As much greatness of mind may be shown in submission as in command, and some women have suffered a life of hardships with as much philosophy as Cato traversed the deserts of Africa, and without that support the view of glory offered him, which is enough for the human mind that is touched with it, to go through any toil or danger. But this is not the situation of a woman whose virtue must only shine to her own recollection, and loses that name when it is ostentatiously exposed to the world. A lady who has performed her duty as a daughter, a wife, and a mother, raises in me as much veneration as Socrates or Xenophon; and much more than I would pay either to Julius Caesar or Cardinal Mazarin, though the first was the most famous enslaver of his own country, and the last the most successful plunderer of his master.

A woman really virtuous, in the utmost extent of this expression, has virtue of a purer kind than any philosopher has ever shown; since she knows, if she has sense, and without it there can be no virtue, that mankind is too much prejudiced against her sex, to give her any degree of that fame which is so sharp a spur to any of their great actions. I have some thoughts of exhibiting a set of pictures of such meritorious ladies, where I shall say nothing of the fire of their eyes, or the pureness of their complexions, but give them such praises as befit a rational sensible being: virtues of choice, and not beauties of accident. I beg they would not so far mistake me, as to think I am undervaluing their charms: a beautiful mind, in a beautiful body, is one of the finest objects shown us by nature. I would not have them place so much value on a quality that can be only useful to one, as to neglect that which may be of benefit to thousands, by precept or by example. There will be no occasion of amusing themselves with trifles, when they consider themselves capable of not only making the most amiable, but the most estimable, figures in life. Begin, then, ladies, by paying those authors with scorn and contempt who, with a sneer of affected admiration, would throw you below the dignity of the human species.

POEMS

JULIA TO OVID

Written at Twelve Years of Age, in imitation of Ovid's Epistles.

Are love and pow'r incapable to meet?
And must they all be wretched who are great?
Enslav'd by titles, and by forms confin'd,
For wretched victims to the state design'd.
What rural maid, that my sad fortune knows,
Would quit her cottage to embrace my woes?
Would be this cursed sacrifice to pow'r,
This wretched daughter of Rome's emperour?
When sick with sighs to absent Ovid given,
I tire with vows the unrelenting Heaven,
Drown'd in my tears, and with my sorrows pale,
What then do all my kindred gods avail?
Let proud Augustus the whole world subdue,
be mine to place all happiness in you;
With nobler pride I can on throes look down,
Can court your love and can despise a crown,—
O Love! thou pleasure never dearly bought!
Whose joys exceed the very lover's thought;
Of that soft passion, when you teach the art,
In gentle sounds it steals into the heart;
With such sweet magic does the soul surprise,
'Tis only taught us better by your eyes.
O Ovid! first of the inspired train,
To Heaven I speak in that enchanting strain,
So sweet a voice can never plead in vain.
Apollo will protect his favourite son,
And all the little Loves unto thy succour run.
The Loves and Muses in thy prayer shall join,
And all their wishes and their vows be thine;

Some god will soften my hard Father's breast,
And work a miracle to make thee blest.

Hard as this is, I even could this bear,
But greater ills than what I feel, I fear.
My fame—my Ovid—both for ever fled,
what greater evil is there left to dread!
Yes, there is one . . . .
Avert it, Gods, who do my sorrows see!
Avert it, thou, who art a god to me!
When back to Rome your wishing eyes are cast,
And on the lessening towers you gaze your last—
When fancy shall recal unto your view
The pleasures now for ever lost to you,
The shining court, and all the thousand ways
To melt the nights and pass the happy days—
Will you not sigh, and hate the wretched maid,
Whose fatal love your safety has betray'd?
Say that from me your banishment does come,
And curse the eyes that have expell'd you Rome?
Those eyes, which now are weeping for your woes,
The sleep of death shall then for ever close.

IRREGULAR VERSES TO TRUTH

Written at Fourteen Years of Age

Where, lovely Goddess, dost thou dwell?
In what remote and silent shade?
Within what cave or lonely cell?
With what old hermit, or unpractis'd maid?
In vain I've sought thee all around,
But thy unfashionable sound
In crowds was never heard,
Nor ever has thy form in town or court appear'd.
The sanctuary is not safe to thee,
Chas'd thence by endless mystery;
Thy own professors chase thee thence,
And wage eternal war with thee and sense;
Then in perplexing comments lost,
E'en when they would be thought to show the most.
Most beautiful when most distress'd,
Descend, O Goddess, to my breast;
There thou may'st reign, unrivall'd and alone,
My thoughts thy subject, and my heart thy throne.

SONG

How happy is the harden'd heart,
Where interest is the only view!
Can sigh and meet, or smile and part,
Nor pleas'd, nor griev'd, nor false, nor true—
Yet, have they truly peace of mind?
Or do they ever truly know
The bliss sincerer tempers find,
Which truth and virtue can bestow?

THE LADY'S RESOLVE

Written on a window, soon after her marriage, 1713

Whilst thirst of praise and vain desire of fame,
In every age is every woman's aim;
With courtship pleas'd, of silly toasters proud,
Fond of a train, and happy in a crowd;
On each proud fop bestowing some kind glance,
Each conquest owing to some loose advance;
While vain coquets affect to be pursued,
And think they're virtuous, if not grossly lewd:
Let this great maxim be my virtue's guide;
In part she is to blame that has been try'd—
He comes too near, that comes to be deny'd.

TOWN ECLOGUES

Written in the Year 1715

MONDAY

ROXANA; OR, THE DRAWING-ROOM

Roxana, from the court retiring late,
Sigh'd her soft sorrows at St. James's gate.
Such heavy thoughts lay brooding in her breast,
Not her own chairmen with more weight oppress'd;
They groan the cruel load they're doom'd to bear;
She in these gentle sounds express'd her care.
"Was it for this that I these roses wear?

For this new-set the jewels for my hair?
Ah! Princess! with what zeal have I pursued!
Almost forgot the duty of a prude.
Thinking I never could attend too soon,
I've miss'd my prayers, to get me dress'd by noon.
For thee, ah! what for thee did I resign?
My pleasures, passions, all that e'er was mine.
I sacrific'd both modesty and ease,
Left operas and went to filthy plays;
Double-entendres shock my tender ear;
Yet even this for thee I choose to bear.
In glowing youth, when nature bids be gay,
And every joy of life before me lay,
By honor prompted, and by pride restrain'd,
The pleasures of the young my soul disdain'd:
Sermons I sought, and with a mien severe
Censur'd my neighbours, and said daily pray'r.
"Alas! how chang'd—with the same sermon-mien
that once I pray'd, the What d'ye call't I've seen.
Ah! cruel Princess, for thy sake I've lost
That reputation which so dear had cost:
I, who avoided every public place,
When bloom and beauty bade me show my face,
Now near thee constant every night abide
With never-failing duty by thy side;
Myself and daughters standing on a row,
To all the foreigners a goodly show!
Oft had your drawing-room been sadly thin,
And merchant's wives close by the chair been seen,
Had I not amply fill'd the empty space,
And sav'd your highness from the dire disgrace.
"Yet Coquetilla's artifice prevails,
When all my merit and my duty fails;
That Coquetilla, whose deluding airs
Corrupt our virgins, still our youth ensnares;
So sunk her character, so lost her fame
Scarce visited before your highness came:
Yet for the bed-chamber 'tis her you choose,
When zeal and fame and virtue you refuse.
Ah! worthy choice! not one of all your train
Whom censure blasts not, and dishonours stain!
Let the nice hind now suckle dirty pigs,
And the proud pea-hen hatch the cuckoo's eggs!
Let Iris leave her paint and own her age,
And grave Suffolka wed a giddy page!
A greater miracle is daily view'd,
A virtuous Princess, with a court so lewd.
"I know thee, court! with all thy treach'rous wiles,

Thy false caresses and undoing smiles!
Ah! Princess, learn'd in all the courtly arts,
To cheat our hopes, and yet to gain our hearts!
"Large lovely bribes are the great statesman's aim;
And the neglected patriot follows fame.
The Prince is ogled; some the King pursue;
But your Roxana only follows you.
Despis'd Roxana, cease, and try to find
Some other, since the Princess proves unkind:
Perhaps it is not hard to find at court,
If not a greater, a more firm support."

TUESDAY.—ST. JAMES'S COFFEE-HOUSE

SILLIANDER AND PATCH

Thou, who so many favours hast receiv'd,
Wond'rous to tell, and hard to be believ'd,
Oh! Hervey, to my lays attention lend,
Hear how two lovers boastingly contend;
Like thee successful, such their bloomy youth,
Renown'd alike for gallantry and truth.
St. James's bell had toll'd some wretches in
(As tatter'd riding-hoods alone could sin),
The happier sinners now their charms recruit,
And to their manteaus their complexion suit;
The opera queens had finish'd half their faces,
And city dames already taken places;
Fops of all kinds, to see the Lion, run;
The beauties stay till the first act's begun,
And beaux stay home to put fresh linen on.
No well-dress'd youth in coffee-house remain'd
But pensive Patch, who on the window lean'd;
And Silliander, that, alert and gay,
First pick'd his teeth, and then began to say:

SILLIANDER
Why all these sighs? ah! why so pensive grown?
Some cause there is why thus you sit alone.
Does hapless passion all this sorrow move?
Or dost thou envy where the ladies love?

PATCH
If, whom they love, my envy must pursue,
'Tis true at least I never envy you.

SILLIANDER

No, I'm unhappy—you are in the right—
'Tis you they favour, and 'tis me they slight.
Yet I could tell, but that I hate to boast,
A club of ladies where 'tis me they toast.

PATCH

Toasting does seldom any favour prove;
Like us, they never toast the thing they love.
A certain duke one night my health begun;
With cheerful pledges round the room it run,
'Till the young Silvia, press'd to drink it too,
Started, and vow'd she knew not what to do:
What, drink a fellow's health! she died with shame
Yet blush'd whenever she pronounc'd my name.

SILLIANDER

Ill fates pursue me, may I never find
The dice propitious, or the ladies kind,
If fair Miss Flippy's fan I did not tear,
And one from me she condescends to wear!

PATCH

Women are always ready to receive;
'Tis then a favour when the sex we give.
A lady (but she is too great to name),
Beauteous in person, spotless in her fame,
With gentle strugglings let me force this ring;
Another day may give another thing.

SILLIANDER

I could say something—see this billet-doux—
And as for presents—look upon my shoe—
These buckles were not forc'd, nor half a theft,
But a young countess fondly made the gift.

PATCH

My countess is more nice, more artful too,
Affects to fly, that I may fierce pursue:
This snuff-box which I begg'd, she still deny'd,
And when I strove to snatch it, seem'd to hide;
She laugh'd and fled, and as I sought to seize,
With affectations cramm'd it down her stays;
Yet hop'd she did not place it there unseen,
I press'd her breasts, and pull'd it from between.

SILLIANDER

Last night, as I stood ogling of her Grace,

Drinking delicious poison from her face,
The soft enchantress did that face decline,
Nor ever rais'd her eyes to meet with mine;
With sudden art some secret did pretend,
Lean'd cross two chairs to whisper to a friend,
While the stiff whalebone with the motion rose,
And thousand beauties to my sight expose.

PATCH
Early this morn—(but I was ask'd to come)
I drank bohea in Celia's dressing-room:
Warm from her bed, to me alone within,
Her night-gown fasten'd with a single pin;
Her night-clothes tumbled with resistless grace,
And her bright hair play'd careless round her face;
Reaching the kettle made her gown unpin,
She wore no waistcoat, and her shift was thin.

SILLIANDER
See Titania driving to the park!
Haste! let us follow, 'tis not yet too dark:
In her all beauties of the spring are seen,
Her cheeks are rosy, and her mantle green.

PATCH
See Tintoretta to the opera goes!
Haste! or the crowd will not permit our bows;
In her the glory of the heav'ns we view,
Her eyes are star-like, and her mantle blue.

SILLIANDER
What color does in Celia's stockings shine?
Reveal that secret, and the prize is thine.

PATCH
What are her garters? Tell me, if you can;
I'll freely own thee far the happier man.
Thus Patch continued his heroic strain,
While Silliander but contends in vain;
After a contest so important gain'd,
Unrivall'd Patch in every ruelle reign'd.

WEDNESDAY.—THE TETE-A-TETE. DANCINDA

"No, fair Dancinda, no; you strive in vain
To calm my care, and mitigate my pain;

If all my sighs, my cares, can fail to move,
Ah! soothe me not with fruitless vows of love."
Thus Strephon spoke. Dancinda thus replied;
"What must I do to gratify your pride?
Too well you know (ungrateful as thou art)
How much you triumph in this tender heart:
"What proof of love remains for me to grant?
Yet still you teaze me with some new complaint.
Oh! would to heaven!—but the fond wish is vain—
Too many favours had not made it plain!
But such a passion breaks through all disguise,
Love reddens on my cheek, and wishes in my eyes.
Is't not enough (inhuman and unkind!)
I own the secret conflict of my mind?
You cannot know what secret pain I prove,
When I, with burning blushes, own I love.
You see my artless joy at your approach,
I sigh, I faint, I tremble at your touch;
And in your absence all the world I shun;
I hate mankind, and curse the cheering sun;
Still as I fly, ten thousand swains pursue;
Ten thousand swains I sacrifice to you.
I show you all my heart without disguise;
But these are tender proofs that you despise—
I see too well what wishes you pursue;
You would not only conquer, but undo:
You, cruel victor, weary of your flame,
Would seek a cure in my eternal shame;
And, not content my honour to subdue,
Now strive to triumph o'er my virtue too.
O Love! a god indeed to womankind,
Whose arrows burn me, and whose fetters bind,
Avenge thy altars, vindicate thy fame,
And blast these traitors that profane thy name
Who, by pretending to thy sacred fire,
Raise cursed trophies to impure desire.
"Have you forgot with what ensnaring art,
You first seduc'd this fond uncautious heart?
Then as I fled, did you not kneeling cry,
'Turn, cruel beauty; whither would you fly?
Why all these doubts? why this distrustful fear?
No impious wishes shall offend your ear:
Nor ever shall my boldest hopes pretend
Above the title of a tender friend;
Blest, if my lovely goddess will permit
My humble vows thus sighing at her feet.
The tyrant, Love, that in my bosom reigns,
The god himself submits to wear your chains;

You shall direct his course, his ardour tame,
And check the fury of his wildest flame.'"
"Unpractis'd youth is easily deceived;
Sooth'd by such sounds I listen'd and believ'd:
Now quite forgot that soft submissive fear,
You dare to ask what I must blush to hear.
"Could I forget the honour of my race,
And meet your wishes, fearless of disgrace;
Could passion o'er my tender youth prevail,
And all my mother's pious maxims fail;
Yet to preserve your heart (which still must be,
False as it is, for ever dear to me)
This fatal proof of love I would not give,
Which you'd contemn the moment you receive.
The wretched she, who yields to guilty joys,
A man may pity, but he must despise.
Your ardour ceas'd, I then should see you shun
The wretched victim by your arts undone.
Yet if I could that cold indifference bear,
What more would strike me with the last despair,
With this reflection would my soul be torn,
To know I merited your cruel scorn.
"Has love no pleasures free from guilt or fear?
Pleasures less fierce, more lasting, more sincere?
Thus let us gently kiss and fondly gaze;
Love is a child, and like a child he plays.
"O Strephon! if you would continue just,
If love be something more than brutal lust,
Forbear to ask what I must still deny,
This bitter pleasure, this destructive joy,
So closely follow'd by this dismal train
Of cutting shame, and guilt's heart-piercing pain."
She paus'd, and fix'd her eye upon her fan!
He took a pinch of snuff, and thus began:
"Madam, if love—" But he could say no more,
For Mademoiselle came rapping at the door.
The dangerous moments no adieus afford:
—"Begone," she cries, "I'm sure I hear my lord."
The lover starts from his unfinish'd loves,
To snatch his hat, and seek his scatter'd gloves:
The sighing dame to meet her dear prepares,
While Strephon, cursing, slips down the back stairs.

THURSDAY.—THE BASSETTE-TABLE

SMILINDA AND CARDELIA

CARDELIA

The Bassette-Table spread, the Tallier come;
Why stays Smilinda in her dressing-room?
Rise, pensive nymph! the Tallier waits for you.

SMILINDA

Ah! madam, since my Sharper is untrue,
I joyless make my once ador'd alpiu.
I joyless saw him stand behind Ombrelia's chair,
And whisper with that soft deluding air,
And those feign'd sighs, which cheat the list'ning fair.

CARDELIA

Is this the cause of your romantic strains?
A mightier grief my heavier heart sustains.
As you by Love, so I by Fortune cross'd,
In one bad deal three septlevas have lost.

SMILINDA

Is that the grief which you compare with mine!
With ease the smiles of Fortune I resign:
Would all my gold in one bad deal were gone;
Were lovely Sharper mine, and mine alone!

CARDELIA

A lover lost is but a common care:
And prudent nymphs against that charge prepare.
The knave of clubs thrice lost: oh! who could guess
This fatal stroke! this unforeseen distress?

SMILINDA

See Betty Loveit, very a propos,
She all the care of love and play does know;
Dear Betty shall th'important point decide;
Betty, who oft the pain of each has try'd;
Impartial she shall say who suffers most,
By cards' ill usage, or by lovers lost.

LOVEIT

Tell, tell your griefs; attentive will I stay,
Though time is precious, and I want some tea.

CARDELIA

Behold this equipage, by Mathers wrought,
With fifty guineas (a great penn'orth!) bought.
See on the toothpick, Mars and Cupid strive;
And both the struggling figures seem alive.

Upon the bottom shines the queen's bright face;
A myrtle foliage round the thimble case.
Jove, jove himself, does on the scissors shine;
The metal, and the workmanship divine!

SMILINDA
This snuff-box, once the pledge of Sharper's love,
When rival beauties for the present strove;
At Corticelli's he the raffle won;
Then first his passion was in public shown:
Hazardia blush'd, and turn'd her head aside,
A rival's envy (all in vain) to hide.
This snuff-box—on the hinge see brilliants shine:
This snuff-box will I stake, the prize is mine.

CARDELIA
Alas! far lesser losses than I bear,
Have made a soldier sigh, a lover swear,
And oh! what makes the disappointment hard,
'Twas my own lord that drew the fatal card.
In complaisance I took the queen he gave,
Though my own secret wish was for the knave.
The knave won Sonica which I had chose;
And the next pull my septleva I lose.

SMILINDA
But ah! what aggravates the killing smart,
The cruel thought that stabs me to the heart;
This curs'd Ombrelia, this undoing fair,
By whose vile arts this heavy grief I bear;
She, at whose name I shed these spiteful tears,
She owes to me the very charms she wears:
An awkward thing when first she came to town;
Her shape unfashion'd, and her face unknown:
She was my friend, I taught her first to spread
Upon her sallow cheeks enlivening red.
I introduc'd her to the park and plays;
And by my int'rest Cosins made her stays.
Ungrateful wretch! with mimic airs grown pert,
She dares to steal my favourite lover's heart.

CARDELIA
Wretch that I was! how often have I swore,
When Winnall tallied, I would punt no more?
I know the bite, yet to my ruin run;
And see the folly which I cannot shun.

SMILINDA

How many minds have Sharper's vows deceiv'd!
How many curs'd the moment they believ'd!
Yet his known falsehoods could no warning prove;
Ah! what is warning to a maid in love?

CARDELIA

But of what marble must that breast be form'd,
To gaze on Bassette, and remain unwarm'd?
When kings, queens, knaves, are set in decent rank,
Expos'd in glorious heaps the tempting bank,
Guineas, half-guineas, all the shining train;
The winner's pleasure, and the loser's pain:
In bright confusion open rouleaus{48} lie,
They strike the soul, and glitter in the eye.
Fir'd by the sight, all reason I disdain:
My passions rise, and will not bear the rein.
Look upon Bassette, you who reason boast;
And see if reason must not there be lost.

SMILINDA

What more than marble must that heart compose,
Can hearken coldly to my Sharper's vows?
Then when he trembles, when his blushes rise,
When awful love seems melting in his eyes,
With eager beats his Mechlin cravat moves:
He loves, I whisper to myself, he loves!
Such unfeign'd passion in his looks appears,
I lose all mem'ry of my former fears:
My panting heart confesses all his charms,
I yield at once, and sink into his arms:
Think of that moment, you who prudence boast,
For such a moment, prudence well were lost.

CARDELIA

At the Groom-Porter's, batter'd bullies play,
Some dukes at Marybone bowl time away.
But who the bowl, or rattling dice, compares
To Bassette's heavenly joys and pleasing cares?

SMILINDA

Soft Simplicetta doats upon a beau;
Prudina likes a man, and laughs at show.
Their several graces in my Sharper meet;
Strong as the footman, as the master sweet.

LOVEIT

Cease your contention, which has been too long
I grow impatient, and the tea too strong.

Attend, and yield to what I now decide;
The equipage shall grace Smilinda's side:
The snuff-box to Cardelia I decree:
Now leave complaining, and begin your tea.

FRIDAY.—THE TOILETTE

LYDIA

Now twenty springs had cloth'd the Park with green,
Since Lydia knew the blossom of fifteen;
No lovers now her morning hours molest,
And catch her at her toilet half undrest.
The thund'ring knocker wakes the street no more,
Nor chairs, nor coaches, crowd the silent door;
Now at the window all her mornings pass,
Or at the dumb devotion of her glass:
Reclin'd upon her arm she pensive sate,
And curs'd th' inconstancy of man too late.
"O youth! O spring of life, for ever lost!
No more my name shall reign the fav'rite toast:
On glass no more the diamond grave my name,
And lines mis-spelt record my lover's flame:
Nor shall side-boxes watch my wand'ring eyes,
And, as they catch the glance, in rows arise
With humble bows; nor white-glov'd beaux encroach
In crowds behind, to guard me to my coach.
"What shall I do to spend the hateful day?
At chapel shall I wear the morn away?
Who there appears at these unmodish hours,
But ancient matrons with their frizzled tow'rs,
And gray religious maids? My presence there,
Amidst that sober train, would own despair?
Nor am I yet so old, nor is my glance
As yet fix'd wholly on devotion's trance.
Strait then I'll dress, and take my wonted range
Through India's shops, to Motteux's, or the Change,
Where the tall jar erects its stately pride,
With antic shapes in China's azure dy'd;
There careless lies a rich brocade unroll'd,
Here shines a cabinet with burnish'd gold.
But then alas! I must be forc'd to pay,
And bring no penn'orth, not a fan away!
"How am I curs'd, unhappy and forlorn!
My lover's triumph, and my sex's scorn!
False is the pompous grief of youthful heirs;

False are the loose coquet's inveigling airs;
False is the crafty courtier's plighted word;
False are the dice when gamesters stamp the board;
False is the sprightly widow's public tear;
Yet these to Damon's oaths are all sincere.
"For what young flirt, base man, am I abus'd?
To please your wife am I unkindly us'd?
'Tis true her face may boast the peach's bloom;
But does her nearer whisper breathe perfume?
I own her taper shape is form'd to please;
But don't you see her unconfin'd by stays?
She doubly to fifteen may claim pretence;
Alike we read it in her face and sense.
Insipid, servile thing! whom I disdain;
Her phlegm can best support the marriage chain.
Damon is practis'd in the modish life,
Can hate, and yet be civil to his wife:
He games, he drinks, he swears, he fights, he roves;
Yet Cloe can believe he fondly loves.
Mistress and wife by turns supply his need;
A miss for pleasure, and a wife for breed.
Powder'd with diamonds, free from spleen or care,
She can a sullen husband's humour bear;
Her credulous friendship and her stupid ease,
Have often been my jest in happier days;
How Chloe boasts and triumphs in my pains!
To her he's faithful; 'tis to me he feigns.
Am I that stupid thing to bear neglect,
And force a smile, not daring to suspect?
No, perjur'd man! a wife may be content;
But you shall find a mistress can resent."
Thus love-sick Lydia rav'd; her maid appears,
And in her faithful hand the band-box bears
(The cestus, that reform'd inconstant Jove,
Not better fill'd with what allur'd to love);
"How well this ribbon's gloss becomes your face!"
She cries in rapture; "then so sweet a lace!
How charmingly you look! so bright! so fair!
"Tis to your eyes the head-dress owes its air!"
Straight Lydia smiled; the comb adjusts her locks;
And at the play-house Harry keeps her box.

SATURDAY.—THE SMALL-POX

FLAVIA

The wretched Flavia, on her couch reclined,
Thus breath'd the anguish of a wounded mind,
A glass revers'd in her right hand she bore,
For now she shunn'd the face she sought before.
"How am I chang'd! alas! how am I grown
A frightful spectre to myself unknown!
Where's my complexion? where my radiant bloom,
That promis'd happiness for years to come?
Then with what pleasure I this face survey'd!
To look once more, my visits oft delay'd!
Charm'd with the view, a fresher red would rise,
And a new life shot sparkling from my eyes!
"Ah! faithless glass, my wonted bloom restore;
Alas! I rave, that bloom is now no more!
The greatest good the gods on men bestow,
Ev'n youth itself, to me is useless now.
There was a time (oh! that I could forget!)
When opera-tickets pour'd before my feet;
And at the Ring, where brightest beauties shine,
The earliest cherries of the spring were mine.
Witness, O Lilly; and thou, Motteux, tell,
How much japan these eyes have made ye sell.
With what contempt ye saw me oft despise
The humble offer of the raffled prize;
For at each raffle still each prize I bore,
With scorn rejected, or with triumph wore!
Now beauty's fled, and presents are no more!
"For me the patriot has the House forsook,
And left debates to catch a passing look:
For me the soldier has soft verses writ:
For me the beau has aim'd to be a wit.
For me the wit to nonsense was betray'd;
The gamester has for me his dun delay'd,
And overseen the card he would have play'd.
The bold and haughty, by success made vain,
Aw'd by my eyes have trembled to complain:
The bashful 'squire, touch'd by a wish unknown,
Has dar'd to speak with spirit not his own:
Fir'd by one wish, all did alike adore;
Now beauty's fled, and lovers are no more!
"As round the room I turn my weeping eyes,
New unaffected scenes of sorrow rise.
Far from my sight that killing picture bear,
The face disfigure, and the canvas tear:
That picture which with pride I us'd to show,
The lost resemblance that upbraids me now.
And thou, my toilette! where I oft have sat,
While hours unheeded pass'd in deep debate

How curls should fall, or where a patch to place;
If blue on scarlet best became my face:
Now on some happier nymph your aid bestow;
On fairer heads, ye useless jewels, glow!
No borrow'd lustre can my charms restore;
Beauty is fled, and dress is now no more!
"Ye meaner beauties, I permit ye shine;
Go, triumph in the hearts that once were mine:
But, 'midst your triumphs with confusion know,
'Tis to my ruin all your charms ye owe.
Would pitying Heav'n restore my wonted mien,
Ye still might move unthought of and unseen:
But oh, how vain, how wretched is the boast
Of beauty faded, and of empire lost!
What now is left but, weeping, to deplore
My beauty fled, and empire now no more!
"Ye cruel chemists, what withheld your aid?
Could no pomatum save a trembling maid?
How false and trifling is that art ye boast!
No art can give me back my beauty lost.
In tears, surrounded by my friends, I lay
Mask'd o'er, and trembled at the sight of day;
Mirmillio came my fortune to deplore
(A golden-headed cane well carv'd he bore),
Cordials, he cried, my spirits must restore!
Beauty is fled, and spirit is no more!
"Galen, the grave officious Squirt was there.
With fruitless grief and unavailing care;
Machaon too, the great Machaon, known
By his red cloak and his superior frown;
And why, he cried, this grief and this despair?
You shall again be well, again be fair;
Believe my oath (with that an oath he swore);
False was his oath; my beauty was no more!
"Cease, hapless maid, no more thy tale pursue,
Forsake mankind, and bid the world adieu!
Monarchs and beauties rule with equal sway:
All strive to serve, and glory to obey:
Alike unpitied when depos'd they grow,
Men mock the idol of their former vow.
"Adieu! ye parks—in some obscure recess,
Where gentle streams will weep at my distress,
Where no false friend will in my grief take part,
And mourn my ruin with a joyful heart;
There let me live in some deserted place,
There hide in shades this lost inglorious face.
Plays, operas, circles, I no more must view!
My toilette, patches, all the world adieu!"

VERSES

Written in the Chiosk of the British Palace, at Pera, overlooking the city of Constantinople, Dec. 26, 1718

Give me, great God! said I, a little farm,
In summer shady, and in winter warm;
Where a clear spring gives birth to murm'ring brooks,
By nature gliding down the mossy rocks.
Not artfully by leaden pipes convey'd,
Or greatly falling in a forc'd cascade,
Pure and unsullied winding through the shade.
All bounteous Heaven has added to my prayer,
A softer climate and a purer air.
Our frozen Isle now chilling winter binds,
Deform'd by rains, and rough with blasting winds;
The wither'd woods grow white with hoary frost,
By driving storms their verdant beauty lost;
The trembling birds their leafless covert shun,
And seek in distant climes a warmer sun:
The water-nymphs their silent urns deplore,
Ev'n Thames, benumb'd, 's a river now no more:
The barren meads no longer yield delight,
By glist'ning snows made painful to the sight
Here summer reigns with one eternal smile,
Succeeding harvests bless the happy soil;
Fair fertile fields, to whom indulgent Heaven
Has ev'ry charm of ev'ry season given.
No killing cold deforms the beauteous year,
The springing flowers no coming winter fear.
But as the parent rose decays and dies,
The infant buds with brighter colours rise,
And with fresh sweets the mother's scent supplies.
Near them the violet grows with odours blest,
And blooms in more than Tyrian purple drest;
The rich jonquils their golden beams display,
And shine in glory's emulating day;
The peaceful groves their verdant leaves retain,
The streams still murmur undefil'd with rain,
And tow'ring greens adorn the fruitful plain.
The warbling kind uninterrupted sing,
Warm'd with enjoyments of perpetual spring.
Here, at my window, I at once survey
The crowded city and resounding sea;
In distant views the Asian mountains rise,

And lose their snowy summits in the skies;
Above these mountains proud Olympus tow'rs,
The parliamental seat of heavenly pow'rs!
New to the sight my ravish'd eyes admire
Each gilded crescent and each antique spire,
The marble mosques, beneath whose ample domes
Fierce warlike sultans sleep in peaceful tombs;
Those lofty structures, once the Christian's boast,
Their names, their beauty, and their honours lost;
Those altars bright with gold and sculpture grac'd,
By barb'rous zeal of savage foes defac'd;
Soph'a alone, her ancient name retains,
Though th' unbeliever now her shrine profanes;
Where holy saints have died in sacred cells,
Where monarchs pray'd, the frantic dervise dwells.
How art thou fall'n, imperial city, low!
Where are thy hopes of Roman glory now?
Where are thy palaces by prelates rais'd?
Where Grecian artists all their skill display'd,
Before the happy sciences decay'd;
So vast, that youthful kings might here reside,
So splendid, to content a patriarch's pride;
Convents where emperors profess'd of old,
The labour'd pillars that their triumphs told;
Vain monuments of them that once were great,
Sunk undistinguis'd by one common fate;
One little spot the tenure small contains,
Of Greek nobility the poor remains;
Where other Helens, with like powerful charms,
Had once engag'd the warring world in arms;
Those names which royal ancestors can boast,
In mean mechanic arts obscurely lost;
Those eyes a second Homer might inspire,
Fix'd at the loom, destroy their useless fire:
Griev'd at a view, which struck upon my mind
The short-liv'd vanity of humankind.
In gaudy objects I indulge my sight,
And turn where Eastern pomp gives gay delight;
See the vast train in various habits drest,
By the bright scimitar and sable vest
The proud vizier distinguish'd o'er the rest!
Six slaves in gay attire his bridle hold,
His bridle rich with gems, and stirrups gold;
His snowy steed adorn'd with costly pride,
Whole troops of soldiers mounted by his side,
These top the plumy crest Arabian coursers guide.
With artful duty all decline their eyes,
No bellowing shouts of noisy crowds arise;

Silence, in solemn state, the march attends,
Till at the dread divan the slow procession ends.
Yet not these prospects all profusely gay,
The gilded navy that adorns the sea,
The rising city in confusion fair,
Magnificently form'd, irregular,
Where woods and palaces at once surprise,
Gardens on gardens, domes on domes arise,
And endless beauties tire the wand'ring eyes,
So soothe my wishes, or so charm my mind,
As this retreat secure from humankind.
No knave's successful craft does spleen excite,
No coxcomb's tawdry splendour shocks my sight,
No mob-alarm awakes my female fear,
No praise my mind, nor envy hurts my ear,
Ev'n fame itself can hardly reach me here;
Impertinence, with all her tattling train,
Fair-sounding flattery's delicious bane;
Censorious folly, noisy party rage,
The thousand tongues with which she must engage
Who dare have virtue in a vicious age.

EPILOGUE TO MARY QUEEN OF SCOTS

Designed to be spoken by Mrs. Oldfield.

What could luxurious woman wish for more,
To fix her joys, or to extend her pow'r?
Their every wish was in this Mary seen,
Gay, witty, youthful, beauteous, and a queen.
Vain, useless blessings with ill-conduct join'd!
Light as the air, and fleeting as the wind.
Whatever poets write, and lovers vow,
Beauty, what poor omnipotence hast thou!
Queen Bess had wisdom, council, power, and laws;
How few espous'd a wretched beauty's cause!
Learn thence, ye fair, more solid charms to prize;
Contemn the idle flatt'rers of your eyes.
The brightest object shines but while 'tis new:
That influence lessens by familiar view.
Monarchs and beauties rule with equal sway,
All strive to serve, and glory to obey;
Alike unpitied when depos'd they grow—
Men mock the idol of their former vow.
Two great examples have been shown today,
To what sure ruin passion does betray;

What long repentance to short joys is due;
When reason rules, what glory must ensue.
If you will love, love like Eliza then;
Love for amusement, like those traitors, men.
Think that the pastime of a leisure hour
She favour'd oft—but never shar'd her pow'r
The traveller by desert wolves pursu'd,
If by his heart the savage foe's subdued,
The world will still the noble act applaud,
Though victory was gain'd by needful fraud.
Such is, my tender sex, our helpless case;
And such the barbarous heart, hid by the begging face;
By passion fir'd, and not withheld by shame,
They cruel hunters are, we trembling game.
Trust me, dear ladies (For I know 'em well),
They burn to triumph, and they sigh to tell:
Cruel to them that yield, cullies{69} to them that sell.
Believe me, 'tis by far the wiser course,
Superior art should meet superior force:
Hear, but be faithful to your int'rest still:
Secure your hearts—then fool with whom you will.

EPILOGUE TO THE TRAGEDY OF CATO

You see in ancient Rome what folly reign'd;
A folly British men would have disdain'd.
Here's none so weak to pity Cato's case,
Who might have liv'd, and had a handsome place;
But rashly vain, and insolently great,
He perish'd by his fault—and not his fate.
Thank Heav'n! our patriots better ends pursue,
With something more than glory in their view.
Poets write morals—priests for martyrs preach—
Neither such fools to practice what they teach.
Though your dear country much you wish to serve,
For bonny Britons 'tis too hard to starve;
Or what's all one, to any generous mind,
From girls, champagne, and gaming, be confin'd;
Portius might well obey his sire's command,
Returning to his small paternal land;
A low estate was ample to support
His private life, far distant from the court!
Far from the crowd of emulating beaux,
Where Martia never wanted birthday clothes.
For you, who live in these more polish'd days,
To spend your money, lo! ten thousand ways;

Dice may run ill, or duns demand their due,
And ways to get (God knows) are very few;
In times so differing, who shall harshly blame
Our modern heroes, not to act the same?

TO A FRIEND ON HIS TRAVELS

From this vile town, immers'd in smoke and care,
To you who brighten in a purer air,
Your faithful friend conveys her tenderest thought
(Though now perhaps neglected and forgot).
May blooming health your wonted mirth restore,
And every pleasure crown your every hour;
Caress'd, esteem'd, and lov'd, your merit known,
And foreign lands admire you, like your own:
Whilst I in silence various fortunes bear,
Distracted with the rage of bosom-war:
My restless fever tears my changeful brain,
With mix'd ideas of delight and pain;
Sometimes soft views my morning dreams employ
In the faint dawn of visionary joy;
Which rigid reason quickly drives away—
I seek the shade and fly from rising day:
In pleasing madness meet some moment's ease,
And fondly cherish my belov'd disease.
If female weakness melt my woman's mind,
At least no weakness in the choice I find,
Not sooth'd to softness by a warbling flute,
Nor the bought merit of a birthday suit;
Not lost my heart by the surprising skill
In opera tunes, in dancing, or quadrille.
The only charm my inclination moves
Is such a virtue, Heaven itself approves!
A soul superior to each vulgar view,
Great, steady, gentle, generous, and true.
How I regret my trifling hours past,
And look with sorrow oe'r the dreary waste!
In false pursuits and vanity bestow'd,
The perfect image of a dirty road;
Through puddles oft, o'er craggy rocks I stray,
A tiresome dull uncomfortable way:
And after toiling long through thick and thin
To reach some meanly mercenary inn,
The bills are high, and very bad the fare,
I curse the wretched entertainment there:
And, jogging on, resolve to stop no more

Where gaudy signs invite me to the door.

TO THE SAME

Though old in ill, the traitor sure should find
Some secret sting transfix his guilty mind.
Though bribes or favour may protect his fame,
Or fear restrain invectives on his name;
None 'quits himself—his own impartial thought
Condemns—and conscience shall record the fault.
Yet more, my friend! your happy state may bear
This disappointment, as below your care.
For what you have, return to Heav'n your thanks;
Few share the prizes, many draw the blanks.
Of breach of promise loudly you complain,
Have you then known the world so long in vain?
Worse than the iron age, our impious times
Have learn'd to laugh at most flagitious crimes.
Are you to know that 'tis a jest to find
Unthinking honesty pervade the mind?
At best, they say, the man is strangely odd
Who keeps his oath, and can believe a God.
This was the cant when Edward held the throne,
Before Spinoza wrote, or Hobbes was known;
When the gilt Bible was the king's delight,
When prayer preceded day, and hymns the night.
Now softening eunuchs sing Italian airs,
The dancing dame to midnight ball repairs.
Now, if an honest man (like you) I view,
Contemning interest, and to virtue true,
I deem, he deviates from Nature's rules,
Like burning hills, or petrifying pools.
I stand astonish'd at the strange portent,
And think some revolution the event;
As all grave heads were startled, as they heard
That a new comet in the west appear'd;
When from a human mother rabbits sprung,
And Ward his pills like hand-grenadoes flung;
When gratis scattering cures amidst the crowd—
A miracle! as Charteris swears aloud—
A greater miracle I daily see,
The ancient faith of Pius reign in thee.
Observe the wretch, who has that faith forsook,
How clear his voice, and how assur'd his look!
Like innocence, and as serenely bold,
Conscious protection of almighty gold!

While thus he reasons, to relieve his fears:
"Oft I've deceiv'd, yet still have kept my ears.
I have been threat'ned for a broken vow,
And yet successively have laugh'd till now,
And will laugh on, my fortune's not the worse,
When starving cullies rail, or vainly curse."
Shall then the villain 'scape? such knaves as he
Be rich and safe, and from all vengeance free?
Consider, friend, but coolly, and you'll find
Revenge the frailty of a feeble mind;
Nor think he 'scapes though he should never feel
The pangs of poison, or the force of steel.
There is a time when conscience shakes the soul,
When Toland's tenets cannot fear control,
When secret anguish fills the anxious breast,
Vacant from business, nor compos'd by rest;
Then dreams invade, the injur'd gods appear
All arm'd with thunder, and awake his fear;
The wretch will start at every flash that flies,
Grow pale at the first murmur of the skies;
Then, if a fever fires corrupted blood,
In every fit he feels the hand of God.
Trembling, and sunk into the last despair,
He dares not offer one repenting prayer;
For how can hope with desperate guilt agree?
And the worst beast is worthier life than he;
This, at the best, will be his certain fate,
Or Heav'n may sooner think his crimes complete.

FRAGMENT TO

Let mules and asses in that circle tread,
And proud of trappings toss a feather'd head;
Leave you the stupid business of the state,
Strive to be happy, and despise the great:
Come where the Graces guide the gentle day,
Where Venus rules amidst her native sea,
Where at her altar gallantries appear,
And even Wisdom dares not show severe.

TO MR. —

For ever blest be that prolific brain
Which can such stores of images contain!
Thus the charg'd trees, with blooming odours crown'd,

Shed their fair blossoms with profusion round;
So swells the brook with heav'n descended rain,
And flows meand'ring on thirsty plain;
Such various talents were by Heav'n design'd
Too vast a treasure for a single mind),
To please, astonish, and instruct mankind.
With a delight not to be told, I view
Themes long exhausted in your hands grow new;
Past all describing your descriptions are,
So full, so just, so bold, yet regular;
The style so varied that it wants a name,
Which, ever differing, ever is the same;
You raise or calm our passions as you please,
The human heart your powerful pen obeys.
When eager Trasimond pursues the course,
We hear the whip, and see the foaming horse;
With Sophronia we have wept and smil'd,
So soon offended—sooner reconcil'd.
Go on, great author! that the world may see
How bright, when from pedantic fetters free,
True genius shines, and shines alone in thee.
Give new editions, with a noble scorn
Of insect critics, who'd obscure thy morn;
Neglect their censures, nor thy work delay,
The owls still sicken at the sight of day.

JOHN DUKE OF MARLBOROUGH

When the proud Frenchman's strong rapacious hand
Spread o'er Europe ruin and command,
Our sinking temples and expiring law
With trembling dread the rolling tempest saw;
Destin'd a province to insulting Gaul,
This genius rose, and stopp'd the ponderous fall.
His temperate valour form'd no giddy scheme,
No victory ras'd him to a rage of fame;
The happy temper of his even mind
No danger e'er could shock, or conquest blind.
Fashion'd alike by Nature and by Art,
To please, engage, and int'rest ev'ry heart.
In public life by all who saw approv'd,
In private hours by all who knew him lov'd.

A CHARACTER

Though a strong vanity may you persuade—
You are not for a politician made;
Your tropes are drawn from Robin Walpole's head,
Your sense is but repeating what he said;
A useful puppy, eminently known,
As proud to father what he will not own,
Some arguments he leaves you to expose,
Some valets flutter in my lord's old clothes.
But should he strip you of his borrow'd sense,
How poorly thin your boasted eloquence!
Know your own talents better, I advise;
Be brisk, yet dull, but aim not to look wise;
In low insipid rhymes place your delight;
Laugh without jests, and without reading write.
Despis'd men, in ladies' ruelles sit,
Where country coquettes bolster up your wit.
May all your minuets applauses meet!
An able coxcomb only in your feet.
By fawning lies, in leagues with court-knaves grow,
And smile on beauties whom you do not know.
Then, acting all the coyness of a lover,
Your no-intrigue endeavour to discover.
Aiming at wit, in many an evil hour,
Have the perpetual will without the power.
Conceit for breeding, rude for easy take,
Horseplay for wit, and noise for mirth mistake.
Love's perfect joys to perfect men belong;
Seek you but the occasion for a song.
Thus to the end of life may you remain
A merry blockhead, treacherous and vain.

AN ANSWER TO A LOVE-LETTER, IN VERSE

Is it to me this sad lamenting strain?
Are Heaven's choicest gifts bestow'd in vain?
A plenteous fortune and a beauteous bride,
Your love rewarded, and content your pride;
Yet, leaving her, 'tis me that you pursue,
Without one single charm—but being new.
How vile is man! How I detest the ways
Of covert falsehood and designing praise!
As tasteless, easier happiness you slight,
Ruin your joy, and mischief your delight.
Why should poor pug (the mimic of your kind)
Wear a rough chain, and be to box confin'd?

Some cup, perhaps, he breaks, or tears a fan,
While moves, unpunish'd, the destroyer man;
Not bound by vows, and unrestrain'd by shame,
In sport you break the heart, and rend the fame.
Not that your art can be successful here,
Th' already plunder'd need no robber fear.
Nor sighs nor charms, nor flattery, can move,
Too well secur'd against a second love.
Once, and but once, that devil charm'd my mind,
To reason deaf, to observation blind,
I idly hop'd (what cannot Love persuade!)
My fondness equall'd and my truth repaid:
Slow to distrust, and willing to believe;
Long hush'd my doubts, I would myself deceive.
But oh! too soon—this tale would ever last—
Sleep on my wrongs, and let me think them past.
For you, who mourn with counterfeited grief,
And ask so boldly, like a begging thief,
May soon some other nymph inflict the pain
You know so well with cruel art to feign.
Though long you've sported with Dan Cupid's dart,
You may see eyes, and you may feel a heart.
So the brisk wits who stop the evening coach,
Laugh at the fear that follows their approach;
With idle mirth and haughty scorn despise
The passenger's pale cheek and staring eyes;
But seiz'd by justice, find a fright no jest,
And all the terror doubled in their breast.

LORD HERVEY TO MR. FOX

So sung the poet in a humble strain,
With empty pockets, and a head in pain,
Where the soft clime inclin'd the soul to rest,
And past'ral images inspir'd the breast.
Apollo listen'd from his heav'nly bower,
And, in his health restor'd, express'd his power.
Pygmalion thus before the Paphian shrine,
With trembling vows address'd the pow'r divine;
Durst hardly make his hopeless wishes known,
And scarce a greater miracle was shown—
Returning vigour glow'd in every vein,
And gay ideas flutter'd in the brain;
Back he returns to breathe his native air,
And all his first resolves are melted there!

AN EPISTLE TO THE EARL OF BURLINGTON

How happy you! who varied joys pursue;
And every hour presents you something new!
Plans, schemes, and models, all Palladio's art,
For six long months have gain'd upon your heart;
Of collonades, of corridors you talk,
The winding staircase and the cover'd walk;
You blend the orders with Vitruvian toil,
And raise with wond'rous joy the fancy'd pile:
But the dull workman's slow-performing hand
But coldly executes his lord's command.
With dirt and mortar soon you grow displeas'd,
Planting succeeds, and avenues are rais'd,
Canals are cut, and mountains level made,
Bow'rs of retreat, and galleries of shade;
The shaven turf presents a lively green;
The bordering flowers in mystic knots are seen:
With studied art on nature you refine—
The spring beheld you warm in this design,
But scarce the cold attacks your fav'rite trees,
Your inclination fails, and wishes freeze:
You quit the grove so lately you admir'd;
With other views your eager hopes are fir'd;
Post to the city you direct your way;
Not blooming paradise could bribe your stay:
Ambition shows you power's brightest side,
'Tis meanly poor in solitude to hide:
Though certain pains attend the cares of state,
A good man owes his country to be great;
Should act abroad the high distinguish'd part,
Or show at least the purpose of his heart.
With thoughts like these the shining courts you seek,
Full of new projects for almost a week;
You then despise the tinsel-glittering snare,
Think vile mankind below a serious care.
Life is too short for any distant aim;
And cold the dull reward of future fame:
Be happy then, while yet you have to live;
And love is all the blessing Heav'n can give.
Fir'd by new passion you address the fair,
Survey the opera as a gay parterre;
Young Chloe's bloom had made you certain prize,
But for a sidelong glance from Celia's eyes:
Your beating heart acknowledges her pow'r;
Your eager eyes her lovely form devour;

You feel the poison swelling in your breast
, And all your soul by fond desire possess'd.
In dying sighs a long three hours are past;
To some assembly with impatient haste,
With trembling hope, and doubtful fear, you move,
Resolv'd to tempt your fate, and own your love:
But there Belinda meets you on the stairs,
Easy her shape, attracting all her airs;
A smile she gives, and with a smile can wound;
Her melting voice hath music in the sound;
Her every motion wears resistless grace;
Wit in her mien, and pleasure in her face:
Here while you vow eternity of love,
Chloe and Celia unregarded move.
Thus on the sands of Afric's burning plains,
However deeply made, no long impress remains;
The slightest leaf can leave its figure there;
The strongest form is scatter'd by the air.
So yielding the warm temper of your mind,
So touch'd by every eye, so toss'd by wind;
Oh! how unlike the Heav'n my soul design'd!
Unseen, unheard, the throng around me move;
Not wishing praise, insensible of love;
No whispers soften, nor no beauties fire;
Careless I see the dance, and coldly hear the lyre.
So num'rous herds are driv'n o'er the rock;
No print is left of all the passing flock:
So sings the wind around the solid stone;
So vainly beat the waves with fruitless moan.
Tedious the toil, and great the workman's care,
Who dare attempt to fix impressions there:
But should some swain, more skilful than the rest,
Engrave his name upon this marble breast,
Not rolling ages could deface that name;
Through all the storms of life 'tis still the same:
Though length of years with moss may shade the ground,
Deep, though unseen, remains the secret wound.

VERSES

Addressed to the Imitator of the First Satire of the Second Book of Horace

In two large columns on thy motley page
Where Roman wit is strip'd with English rage;
Where ribaldry to satire makes pretence,
And modern scandal rolls with ancient sense:

Whilst on one side we see how Horace thought,
And on the other how he never wrote;
Who can believe, who view the bad, the g
ood, That the dull copyist better understood
That spirit he pretends to imitate,
Than heretofore that Greek he did translate?
Thine is just such an image of his pen,
As thou thyself art of the sons of men,
Where our own species in burlesque we trace,
A sign-post likeness of the human race,
That is at once resemblance and disgrace.
Horace can laugh, is delicate, is clear,
You only coarsely rail, or darkly sneer;
His style is elegant, his diction pure,
Whilst none thy crabbed numbers can endure;
Hard as thy heart, and as thy birth obscure.
If he has thorns, they all on roses grow;
Thine like thistles, and mean brambles show;
With this exception, that, though rank the soil,
Weeds as they are, they seem produc'd by toil.
Satire should, like a polish'd razor, keen,
Wound with a touch, that's scarcely felt or seen:
Thine is an oyster-knife, that hacks and hews;
The rage, but not the talent to abuse;
And is in hate, what love is in the stews.
'Tis the gross lust of hate, that still annoys,
Without distinction, as gross love enjoys:
Neither to folly, nor to vice confin'd,
The object of thy spleen is humankind:
It preys on all who yield, or who resist:
To thee 'tis provocation to exist.
But if thou seest{83} a great and generous heart,
Thy bow is doubly bent to force a dart.
Nor dignity nor innocence is spar'd,
Nor age, nor sex, nor thrones, nor graves, rever'd.
Nor only justice vainly we demand,
But even benefits can't rein thy hand;
To this or that alike in vain we trust,
Nor find thee less ungrateful than unjust.
Not even youth and beauty can control
The universal rancour of thy soul;
Charms that might soften superstition's rage,
Might humble pride, or thaw the ice of age.
But how should'st thou by beauty's force be mov'd,
No more for loving made than to be lov'd?
It was the equity of righteous Heav'n,
That such a soul to such a form was giv'n;
And shows the uniformity of fate,

That one so odious should be born to hate.
When God created thee, one would believe
He said the same as to the snake of Eve;
To human race antipathy declare,
'Twixt them and thee be everlasting war.
But oh! the sequel of the sentence dread,
And whilst you bruise their heel, beware your head.
Nor think thy weakness shall be thy defence,
The female scold's protection in offence.
Sure 'tis as fair to beat who cannot fight,
As 'tis to libel those who cannot write.
And if thou draw'st thy pen to aid the law,
Others a cudgel, or a rod, may draw.
If none with vengeance yet thy crimes pursue,
Or give thy manifold affronts their due;
If limbs unbroken, skin without a stain,
Unwhipt, unblanketed, unkick'd, unslain,
That wretched little carcase you retain,
The reason is, not that the world wants eyes,
But thou'rt so mean, they see, and they despise:
When fretful porcupine, with ranc'rous will,
From mounted back shoots forth a harmless quill,
Cool the spectators stand; and all the while
Upon the angry little monster smile.
Thus 'tis with thee:—while impotently safe,
You strike unwounding, we unhurt can laugh.
Who but must laugh, this bully when he sees,
A puny insect shiv'ring at a breeze?
One over-match'd by every blast of wind,
Insulting and provoking all mankind.
Is this the thing to keep mankind in awe,
To make those tremble who escape the law?
Is this the ridicule to live so long,
The deathless satire and immortal song?
No: like the self-blown praise, thy scandal flies;
And, as we're told of wasps, it stings and dies.
If none do yet return th'intended blow,
You all your safety to your dulness owe:
But whilst that armour thy poor corse defends,
'Twill make thy readers few, as are thy friends:
Those, who thy nature loath'd, yet lov'd thy art,
Who lik'd thy head, and yet abhorr'd thy heart:
Chose thee to read, but never to converse,
And scorn'd in prose him whom they priz'd in verse
Ev'n they shall now their partial error see,
Shall shun thy writings like thy company;
And to thy books shall ope their eyes no more
Than to thy person they would do their door.

Nor thou the justice of the world disown,
That leaves thee thus an outcast and alone;
For though in law to murder be to kill,
In equity the murder's in the will:
Then whilst with coward-hand you stab a name,
And try at least t'assassinate our fame,
Like the first bold assassin's be thy lot,
Ne'er be thy guilt forgiven, or forgot;
But, as thou hat'st be hated by mankind,
And with the emblem of thy crooked mind
Mark'd on thy back, like Cain by God's own hand,
Wander, like him, accursed through the land.

UNFINISHED SKETCHES (of a Larger Poem)

Now, with fresh vigour, morn her light displays,
And the glad birds salute her kindling rays;
The opening buds confess the sun's return,
And rous'd from night all nature seems new-born;
When ponderous Dulness{84} slowly wing'd her way,
And with thick fogs oppos'd the rising day.
Phoebus retir'd as from Thyestes'{85} feast,
Droop'd all the flow'rs, th'aerial music ceas'd.
Pleas'd with her influence, she exults with pride,
"Shall mortal then escape my power?" she cried:
"Nay, in this town where smoke and mists conspire
To cloud the head, and damp the poet's fire,
Shall Addison{86} my empire here dispute,
So justly founded, lov'd, and absolute?
Explode my children, ribaldry and rhyme,
Rever'd from Chaucer's down to Dryden's time?
Distinguish 'twixt false humour and the true,
And wit make lovely to the vulgar view?
No—better things my destiny ordains,
For Oxford has the wand, and Anna reigns."{87}
She ended, and assum'd Duke Disney's{88} grin,
With broad plump face, pert eyes, and ruddy skin,
Which show'd the stupid joke which lurk'd within.
In this lov'd form she knock'd at St. John's gate,
Where crowds already for his levee wait;
And wait they may, those wretches that appear
To talk of service past and long arrear:
But the proud partner of his pleasure goes
Through crowds of envious eyes and servile bows.
And now approaching where the statesman lay,
To his unwilling eyes reveal'd the day.

Starting, he wak'd, and waking swore by God,
"This early visit, friend, is wondrous odd!
Scarce have I rested two small hours in bed,
And fumes of wine oppress my aching head.
By thee I'm sure my soul is understood
Too well to plague me for the public good.
Let stupid patriots toil to serve the brutes,
And waste the fleeting hours in vain disputes;
The use of pow'r supreme I better know,
Nor will I lose the joys the gods bestow;
The sparkling glass, soft flute, and willing fair
Alternate guard me from the shocks of care.
'Tis the prerogative of wit like mine
To emulate in ease the pow'rs divine;
And while I revel, leave the busy fools
To plot like chemists, or to trudge like to
ols." "Believe me, lord! (replies his seeming friend)
Some difficulties every state attend.
Cares must surround the men that wealth possess,
And sorrow mingles ev'n with love's success.
Great as you are, no greatness long is sure,
Advancement is but pain if not secure.
All your long schemes may vanish in an hour,
Oh tremble at the sad reverse of pow'r!
How will these slaves that waiting watch your eye
Insulting smile or pass regardless by!
Nor is this thought the creature of my fears,
Approaching ruin now most strong appears.
Men must be dull who passively obey,
And ignorance fixes arbitrary sway;
Think of this maxim, and no more permit
A dangerous writer to retail his wit.
The consequence of sense is liberty,
And if men think aright, they will be free;
Encourage you the poet I shall bring,
Your Granville, he already tries to sing;
Nor think, my lord, I only recommend
An able author, but a useful friend;
In verse his phlegm, in puns he shows his fi
re, And skill'd in pimping to your heart's desire."
"I thank thee, duke (replies the drowsy peer),
But cannot listen to thy childish fear.
This Addison, 'tis true, debauch'd in schoo
ls, Will sometimes oddly talk of musty rules.
Yet here and there I see a master line,
I feel and I confess the pow'r divine.
In spite of interest charm'd into applause,
I wish for such a champion in our cause:

Nor shall your reasons force me to submit
To patronise a bard of meaner wit;
Men can but say wit did my judgment blind,
And wit's the noblest frailty of the mind."
The disappointed goddess, swell'd with spite,
Dropping her borrow'd form, appears in open light.
So the sly nymph in masquerade disguise,
The faith of her suspected lover tries;
But when the perjury too plain appears,
Her eyes are fill'd with mingled rage and tears;
No more remembers the affected tone,
Sinks the feign'd voice, and thunders in her own.
"How hast thou dar'd my party then to quit,
Or dost thou, wretch, presume thou art a wit?
Read thy own works, consider well each line,
In each dull page, how palpably I shine!
'Tis I that to thy eloquence affords
Such empty thoughts wrapt in superfluous words;
To me alone your pamphlet-praise you owe,
'Tis I your tropes and florid sense bestow;
After such wreaths bestow'd, such service done,
Dare you refuse protection to my son?
The time shall come, though now at court ador'd,
When still a writer, though no more a lord,
On common stalls thy darling works be spread,
And thou shalt answer them to make them read."
She said, and turning show'd her wrinkled neck,
In scales and colour like a roach's back.

THE COURT OF DULNESS

A Fragment

Her palace plac'd beneath a muddy road,
And such the influence of the dull abode,
The carrier's horse above can scarcely drag his load.
Here chose the goddess her belov'd retreat,
Which Pho&ebus tries in vain to penetrate;
Adorn'd within with shells of small expense,
(Emblems of tinsel rhyme and trifling sense),
Perpetual fogs enclose the sacred cave,
The neighbouring sinks their fragrant odours gave;
In contemplation here she pass'd her hours,
Closely attended by subservient powers:
Bold Profanation with a brazen brow,—
Much to this great ally does Dulness owe:

But still more near the goddess you attend,
Naked Obscenity! her darling friend.
To thee for shelter all the dull still fly,
Pert double meanings e'en at school we try.
What numerous writers owe their praise to thee,
No sex—no age—is from thy influence free;
By thee how bright appears the senseless song,
By thee the book is sold, the lines are strong.
The heaviest poet, by thy pow'rful aid,
Warms the brisk youth and charms the sprightly maid;
Where breathes the mortal who's not prov'd thy force
In well-bred pun, or waiting-room discourse?
Such were the chiefs who form'd her gloomy court,
Her pride, her ornaments, and her support:
Behind attended such a numerous crowd
Of quibbles strain'd old rhymes, and laughter loud,
Throngs that might even make a goddess proud.
Yet pensive thoughts lay brooding in her breast,
And fear, the mate of pow'r, her mind oppress'd.
Oft she revolv'd—for oh, too well she knew
What Merlin sung, and part long since prov'd true,
"When Harry's brows the diadem adorn
From Reformation Learning shall be born;
Slowly in strength the infant shall improve,
The parents' glory and its country's love:
Free from the thraldom of monastic rhymes,
In bright progression bless succeeding times;
Milton free poetry from the monkish chain,
And Addison that Milton shall explain;
Point out the beauties of each living page;
Reform the taste of a degen'rate age;
Show that true wit disdains all little art,
And can at once engage and mend the heart;
Knows even popular applause to gain,
Yet not malicious, wanton, or profane."
This prophecy perplex'd her anxious head;
And, yawning thrice, thus to her sons she said:
"When such an author honour'd shall appear,
'Tis plain, the hour of our destruction's near!
And public rumour now aloud proclaims
At universal monarchy he aims.
What to this hero, whom shall we oppose?
A strong confederacy of stupid foes—
Such brave allies as are by nature fit
To check the progress of o'erflowing wit;
Where envy and where impudence are join'd
To contradict the voice of humankind,
At Dacier's ignorance shall gravely smile,

And blame the coarseness of Spectator's style;
Shall swear that Tickell understands not Greek,
That Addison can't write, nor Walpole speak."
Fir'd by this project Profanation rose—
"One leader, Goddess, let me here propose;
In a near realm, which owns thy gentle sway,
My darling son now chants his pleasing lay,
Trampling on order, decency, and laws,
And vaunts himself the champion of my cause.
Him will I bring to teach the callow youth
To scorn dry morals—laugh at sacred truth.
All fears of future reckonings he shall quench,
And bid them bravely drink and freely wench.
By his example much, by precept more,
There learn 'tis wit to swear, and safe to whore.

Mocks Newton's schemes, and Tillotson's discourse,
And imitates the virtues of a horse.
With this design to add to his renown,
He wears the rev'rend dress of band and gown."
The Goddess, pleas'd, bestow'd a gracious grin,
When thus does fair Obscenity begin:
"My humbler subjects are not plac'd so high,
They joke in kitchens, and in cellars ply;
Yet one I have, bred in those worthy schools,
Admir'd by shoals of male and female fools;
In ballads what I dictate he shall sing,
And troops of converts to my banners bring.
Bold in my cause, and most profoundly dull,
With smooth unmeaning rhymes the town shall lull;
Shall sing of worms in great Arbuthnot's strain,
In lewd burlesque the sacred Psalms profane;
To maids of honour songs obscene address,
Nor need we doubt his wonderful success.
Long have I watch'd this genius yet unknown,
Inspir'd his rhyme, and mark'd him for my own;
His early youth in superstition bred,
And monkish legends all the books he read.
Tinctur'd by these, proceeds his love of rhyme,
Milton he scorns, but Crambo thinks divine.
And oh! 'tis sure (our foes confess this truth)
The old Cambronians yield to this stupendous youth.
But present want obscures the poet's name,
Be it my charge to talk him into fame.
My Lansdowne (whose love-songs so smoothly run,
My darling author, and my fav'rite son)
He shall protect the man whom I inspire,
And Windsor Forest openly admire;

And Bolingbroke with flattery shall bribe,
'Till the charm'd lord most nobly shall subscribe;
And hostile Addison too late shall find,
'Tis easier to corrupt than mend mankind.
The town, which now revolts, once more obey,
And the whole island own my pristine sway!"
She said, and slowly leaves the realm of night,
While the curs'd phantoms praise her droning flight.

AN EPISTLE FROM POPE TO LORD BOLINGBROKE

Confess, dear La&elius! pious, just, and wise,
Some self-content does in that bosom rise,
When you reflect, as sure you sometimes must,
What talents Heaven does to thy virtue trust,
While with contempt you view poor humankind,
Weak, wilful, sensual, passionate, and blind.
Amid these errors thou art faultless found,
(The moon takes lustre from the darkness round)
Permit me too, a small attendant star,
To twinkle, though in a more distant spher
e; Small things with great, we poets oft compare.
With admiration all your steps I view,
And almost envy what I can't pursue.
The world must grant (and 'tis no common fame)
My courage and my probity the same.
But you, great Lord, to nobler scenes were born;
Your early youth did Anna's court adorn.
Let Oxford own, let Catalonia tell,
What various victims to your wisdom fell;
Let vows or benefits the vulgar bind,
Such ties can never chain th'intrepid mind.
Recorded be that memorable hour,
When, to elude exasperated pow'r
With blushless front you durst your friend betray,
Advise the whole confed'racy to stay,
While with sly courage you run brisk away.
By a deserted court with joy receiv'd,
Your projects all admir'd, your oaths believ'd;
Some trust obtain'd, of which good use he made,
To gain a pardon where you first betray'd.
But what is pardon to th'aspiring breast?
You should have been first minister at least:
Failing of that, forsaken and depress'd,
Sure any soul but yours had sought for rest!
And mourn'd in shades, far from the public eye,

Successless fraud, and useless infamy.
And here, my lord! let all mankind admire
The efforts bold of unexhausted fire;
You stand the champion of the people's cause,
And bid the mob reform defective laws.
Oh! was your pow'r, like your intention good,
Your native land would stream with civic blood.
I own these glorious schemes I view with pain;
My little mischiefs to myself seem mean,
Such ills are humble though my heart is great,
All I can do is flatter, lie, and cheat;
Yet I may say 'tis plain that you preside
O'er all my morals, and 'tis much my pride
To tread with steps unequal where you guide.
My first subscribers I have first defam'd,
And when detected, never was asham'd;
Rais'd all the storms I could in private life,
Whisper'd the husband to reform the wife;
Outwitted Lintot in his very trade,
And charity with obloquy repaid.
Yet while you preach in prose, I scold in rhymes,
Against th'injustice of flagitious times.
You, learned doctor of the public stage,
Give gilded poison to corrupt the age;
Your poor toad-eater I, around me scatter
My scurril jests, and gaping crowds bespatter.
This may seem envy to the formal fools
Who talk of virtue's bounds and honour's rules;
We, who with piercing eyes look nature through,
We know that all is right in all we do.
Reason's erroneous—honest instinct right—
Monkeys were made to grin, and fleas to bite.
Using the spite by the Creator given,
We only tread the path that's mark'd by Heaven.
And sure with justice 'tis that we exclaim,
Such wrongs must e'en your modesty inflame;
While blockheads, court-rewards and honours share,
You, poet, patriot, and philosopher,
No bills in pockets, nor no garter wear.
When I see smoking on a booby's board
Fat ortolans and pye of Perigord,
Myself am mov'd to high poetic rage
(The Homer and the Horace of the age),
Puppies who have the insolence to dine
With smiling beauties, and with sparkling wine;
While I retire, plagu'd with an empty purse,
Eat brocoli, and kiss my ancient nurse.
But had we flourish'd when stern Harry reign'd,

Our good designs had been but ill explained;
The axe had cut your solid reas'nings short,
I, in the porter's lodge, been scourg'd at court.
To better times kind Heav'n reserv'd our birth.
Happy for you such coxcombs are on earth!
Mean spirits seek their villainy to hide;
We show our venom'd souls with nobler pride,
And in bold strokes have all man kind defy'd,
Pass'd o'er the bounds that keep mankind in awe,
And laugh'd at justice, liberty, and law.
While our admirers stare with dumb surprise,
Treason and scandal we monopolise.
Yet this remains our most peculiar boast,
You 'scape the block, and I the whipping-post.

LADY HERTFORD (to Lord William Hamilton)

Dear Colin, prevent my warm blushes,
Since how can I speak without pain?
My eyes oft have told you my wishes,
Why don't you their meaning explain?

My passion will lose by expression,
And you may too cruelly blame;
Then do not expect a confession
Of what is too tender to name.

Since yours is the province of speaking,
How can you then hope it from me?
Our wishes should be in our keeping,
'Till yours tell us what they should be.

Alas! then, why don't you discover?
Did your heart feel such torments as mine,
Eyes need not tell over and over,
What I in my breast would confine.

ANSWERED, FOR LORD WILLIAM HAMILTON (by Lady M. W. Montagu)

Good Madam, when ladies are willing,
A man must needs look like a fool;
For me, I would not give a shilling
For one who would love out of rule.

You should leave us to guess by your blushing,
And not speak the matter so plain;
'Tis ours to write and be pushing,
'Tis yours to affect a disdain.

That you're in a terrible taking,
By all these sweet oglings I see;
But the fruit that can fall without shaking,
Indeed is too mellow for me.

EPISTLE FROM ARTHUR GREY, THE FOOTMAN

(To Mrs. Murray after his condemnation for attempting to commit violence)

Read, lovely nymph, and tremble not to read,
I have no more to wish, nor you to dread;
I ask not life, for life to me were vain,
And death a refuge from severer pain.
My only hope in these last lines I try—
I would be pitied, and I then would die.
Long had I liv'd as sordid as my fate,
Nor curs'd the destiny that made me wait
A servile slave: content with homely food,
The gross instinct of happiness pursued:
Youth gave me sleep at night and warmth of blood.
Ambition yet had never touch'd my breast;
My lordly master knew no sounder rest;
With labour healthy, in obedience blest.
But when I saw—oh! had I never seen
That wounding softness, that engaging mien!
The mist of wretched education flies,
Shame, fear, desire, despair, and love arise,
The new creation of those beauteous eyes.
But yet that love pursu'd no guilty aim;
Deep in my heart I hid the secret flame:
I never hop'd my fond desire to tell,
And all my wishes were to serve you well.
Heav'ns! how I flew when wing'd by your command,
And kiss'd the letters giv'n me by your hand.
How pleas'd, how proud, how fond I was to wait,
Present the sparkling wine, or change the plate!
How, when you sung, my soul devour'd the sound,
And ev'ry sense was in the rapture drown'd!
Though bid to go, I quite forgot to move;
—You knew not that stupidity was love!
But oh! the torment not to be express'd,

The grief, the rage, the hell, that fir'd this breast,
When my great rivals, in embroidery gay,
Sate by your side, or led you from the play!
I still contriv'd near as I could to stand
(the flambeau trembling in my shaking hand);
I saw, or thought I saw, those fingers press'd,
For thus their passion by my own I guess'd,
And jealous fury all my soul possess'd.
Like torrents, love and indignation meet,
And madness would have thrown me at your feet.
Turn, lovely nymph (for so I would have said),
Turn from those triflers who make love a trade;
This is true passion in my eyes you see;
They cannot, no—they cannot love like me;
Frequent debauch has pall'd their sickly taste,
Faint their desire, and in a moment past;
They sigh not from the heart, but from the brain;
Vapours of vanity and strong champagne.
Too dull to feel what forms like yours inspire,
After long talking of their painted fire,
To some lewd brothel they at night retire;
There, pleas'd with fancy'd quality and charms,
Enjoy your beauties in a strumpet's arms.
Such are the joys those toasters have in view,
And such the wit and pleasure they pursue;
—And is this love that ought to merit you?
Each opera night a new address begun,
They swear to thousands what they swear to one.
Not thus I sigh—but all my sighs are vain—
Die, wretched Arthur, and conceal thy pain:
'Tis impudence to wish, and madness to complain.
Fix'd on this view, my only hope of ease,
I waited not the aid of slow disease;
The keenest instruments of death I sought,
And death alone employ'd my lab'ring thought.
This all the night—when I remember well
The charming tinkle of your morning bell!
Fir'd by the sound, I hasten'd with your tea,
With one last look to smooth the darksome way—
But oh! how dear that fatal look has cost!
In that fond moment my resolves were lost.
Hence all my guilt, and all your sorrows rise—
I saw the languid softness of your eyes;
I saw the dear disorder of your bed;
Your cheeks all glowing with a tempting red;
Your night-clothes tumbled with resistless grace,
Your flowing hair play'd careless down your face
Your night-gown fasten'd with a single pin;

—Fancy improv'd the wondrous charms within!
I fix'd my eyes upon that heaving breast,
And hardly, hardly, I forbore the rest:
Eager to gaze, unsatisfied with sight,
My head grew giddy with the near delight!
—Too well you know the fatal following night!
Th'extremest proof of my desire I give,
And since you will not love, I will not live.
Condemn'd by you, I wait the righteous doom.
Careless and fearless of the woes to come.
But when you see me waver in the wind,
My guilty flame extinct, my soul resign'd,
Sure you may pity what you can't approve,
The cruel consequence of furious love.
Think the bold wretch, that could so greatly dare,
Was tender, faithful, ardent, and sincere;
Think when I held the pistol to your breast,—
Had I been of the world's large rule possess'd,—
That world had then been yours, and I been blest;
Think that my life was quite below my care,
Nor fear'd I any hell beyond despair.—
If these reflections, though they seize you late,
Give some compassion for your Arthur's fate:
Enough you give, nor ought I to complain:
You pay my pangs, nor have I died in vain.

THE FOURTH ODE OF THE FIRST BOOK OF HORACE IMITATED

"Solvitur acris hyems grata vice veris," &c.

Sharp winter now dissolv'd, the linnet sing,
The grateful breath of pleasing Zephyrs bring
The welcome joys of long-desired spring.
The galleys now for open sea prepare,
The herds forsake their stalls for balmy air,
The fields adorn'd with green th'approaching sun declare.
In shining nights the charming Venus leads
Her troop of Graces, and her lovely maids,
Who gaily trip the ground in myrtle shades.
The blazing forge her husband Vulcan heats
And thunderlike the labouring hammer beats,
While toiling Cyclops every stroke repeats.
Of myrtle new the cheerful wreath compose,
Of various flowers which opening spring bestows,
Till coming June presents the blushing rose.
Pay your vow'd offering to God Faunus' bower!

Then, happy Sestius, seize the present hour,
'Tis all that nature leaves to mortal power.
The equal hand of strong impartial Fate
Levels the peasant and th' imperious great,
Nor will that doom on human projects wait.
To the dark mansions of the senseless dead,
With daily steps our destin'd path we tread,
Realms still unknown, of which so much is said.
Ended your schemes of pleasure and of pride,
In joyous feasts no one will there preside,
Torn from your Lycidas' beloved side.
Whose tender youth does now our eyes engage,
And soon will give, in his maturer age,
Sighs to our virgins—to our matrons rage.

THE FIFTH ODE OF THE FIRST BOOK OF HORACE IMITATED

"Quis multa gracilis te puer in rosa."

For whom are now your airs put on,
And what new beauty's doom'd to be undone?
That careless elegance of dress,
This essence that perfumes the wind,
Your ev'ry motion does confess
Some secret conquest is design'd.

Alas! the poor unhappy maid,
To what a train of ills betray'd!
What fears, what pangs shall rend her breast,
How will her eyes dissolve in tears!
That now with glowing joy is bless'd,
Charm'd with the faithless vows she hears.

So the young sailor on the summer sea
Gaily pursues his destin'd way:
Fearless and careless on the deck he stands,
Till sudden storms arise and thunders roll;
In vain he casts his eyes to distant lands,
Distracting terror tears his timorous soul.

For me, secure I view the raging main,
Past are my dangers, and forgot my pain:
My votive tablet in the temple shows
The monument of folly past;
I paid the bounteous god my grateful vows,
Who snatch'd from ruin, sav'd me at the last.

THE LOVER: A BALLAD

To Mr. Congreve.

At length, by so much importunity press'd,
Take, Congreve, at once the inside of my breast.
This stupid indiff'rence so oft you blame,
Is not owing to nature, to fear, or to shame:
I am not as cold as a virgin in lead,
Nor are Sunday's sermons so strong in my head:
I know but too well how time flies along,
That we live but few years, and yet fewer are young.

But I hate to be cheated, and never will buy
Long years of repentance for moments of joy.
Oh! was there a man (but where shall I find
Good sense and good-nature so equally join'd?)
Would value his pleasure, contribute to mine;
Not meanly would boast, nor lewdly design;
Not over severe, yet not stupidly vain,
For I would have the power, though not give the pain.

No pedant, yet learned; no rake-helly gay,
Or laughing, because he has nothing to say;
To all my whole sex obliging and free,
Yet never be fond of any but me;
In public preserve the decorum that's just,
And show in his eyes he is true to his trust!
Then rarely approach, and respectfully bow,
But not fulsomely pert, nor yet foppishly low.

But when the long hours of public are past,
And we meet with champagne and a chicken at last,
May every fond pleasure that moment endear;
Be banish'd afar both discretion and fear!
Forgetting or scorning the airs of the crowd,
He may cease to be formal, and I to be proud,
Till lost in the joy, we confess that we live,
And he may be rude, and yet I may forgive.

And that my delight may be solidly fix'd,
Let the friend and the lover be handsomely mix'd;
In whose tender bosom my soul may confide,
Whose kindness can soothe me, whose counsel can guide.
From such a dear lover as I here describe,

No danger should fright me, no millions should bribe;
But till this astonishing creature I know,
As I long have liv'd chaste, I will keep myself so.

I never will share with the wanton coquette,
Or be caught by a vain affectation of wit.
The toasters and songsters may try all their art,
But never shall enter the pass of my heart.
I loathe the lewd rake, the dress'd fopling despise:
Before such pursuers the nice virgin flies;
And as Ovid has sweetly in parable told,
We harden like trees, and like rivers grow cold.

ON SEEING A PORTRAIT OF SIR ROBERT WALPOLE

Such were the lively eyes and rosy hue
Of Robin's face, when Robin first I knew;
The gay companion and the fav'rite guest;
Lov'd without awe, and without views caress'd;
His cheerful smile, and open honest look,
Added new graces to the truth he spoke.
Then ev'ry man found something to commend,
The pleasant neighbour and the worthy friend;
The gen'rous master of a private house,
The tender father and indulgent spouse.
The hardest censors at the worst believ'd,
His temper was too easily deceiv'd
(A consequential ill good-nature draws,
A bad effect, but from a noble cause).
Whence, then, these clamours of a judging crowd?
Suspicious, griping, insolent, and proud—
Rapacious, cruel, violent, unjust;
False to his friend, and traitor to his trust?

AN ELEGY ON MRS. THOMPSON

Unhappy fair, by fatal love betray'd!
Must then thy beauties thus untimely fade!
And all thy blooming, soft, inspiring charms,
Become a prey to Death's destructive arms!
Though short thy day, and transient like the wind,
How far more blest than those yet left behind!
Safe in the grave thy griefs with thee remain;
And life's tempestuous billows break in vain.

Ye tender nymphs in lawless pastimes gay,
Who heedless down the paths of pleasures stray;
Though long secure, with blissful joys elate,
Yet pause and think of Arabella's fate;
For such may be your unexpected doom,
And your next pleasures lull you in the tomb.
But let it be the muse's gentle care
To shield from envy's rage the mould'ring fair;
To draw a veil o'er faults she can't defend;
And what prudes have devour'd, leave time to end:
Be it her part to drop a pitying tear,
And mourning sigh around thy sable bier,
Nor shall thy woes long glad th'ill-natur'd crowd,
Silent to praise, and in detraction loud:
When scandal, that through life each worth destroys,
And malice that embitters all our joys,
Shall in some ill-starr'd wretch find later stains,
And let thine rest, forgot as thy remains.

ON THE DEATH OF MRS. BOWLES

Written extempore on a card, in a large company, December 14, 1724

Hail, happy bride, for thou art truly blest!
Three months of rapture, crown'd with endless rest.
Merit like yours was Heav'n's peculiar care,
You lov'd—yet tasted happiness sincere.
To you the sweets of love were only shown,
The sure succeeding bitter dregs unknown;
You had not yet the fatal charge deplor'd,
The tender lover for th'imperious lord:
Nor felt the pain that jealous fondness brings:
Nor felt, that coldness from possession springs.
Above your sex, distinguish'd in your fate,
You trusted—yet experienc'd no deceit;
Soft were your hours, and wing'd with pleasure flew;
No vain repentance gave a sigh to you:
And if superior bliss Heaven can bestow,
With fellow-angels you enjoy it now.

A MAN IN LOVE

"L'Homme qui ne se trouve point, et ne se trouvera jamais."

The man who feels the dear disease,
Forgets himself, neglects to please,
The crowd avoids, and seeks the groves,
And much he thinks when much he loves;
Press'd with alternate hope and fear,
Sighs in her absence, sighs when near.
The gay, the fond, the fair, the young,
Those trifles pass unseen along,
To him a pert insipid throng.
But most he shuns the vain coquette;
Contemns her false affected wit:
The minstrel's sound, the flowing bowl,
Oppress and hurt the amorous soul.
'Tis solitude alone can please,
And give some intervals of ease.
He feeds the soft distemper there,
And fondly courts the distant fair;
To balls the silent shade prefers,
And hates all other charms but hers.
When thus your absent swain can do,
Molly, you may believe him true.

A BALLAD

To the tune of "The Irish Howl."

To that dear nymph, whose pow'rful name
Does every throbbing nerve inflame
(As the soft sound I low repeat,
My pulse unequal measures beat),
Whose eyes I never more shall see,
That once so sweetly shin'd on thee;
Go, gentle wind! and kindly bear
My tender wishes to the fair.
Hoh, ho, ho, &c.

Amidst her pleasures let her know
The secret anguish of my woe,
The midnight pang, the jealous hell,
Does in this tortur'd bosom dwell:
While laughing she, and full of play,
Is with her young companions gay;
Or hearing in some fragrant bower
Her lover's sigh, and beauty's power.
Hoh, ho, ho, &c.

Lost and forgotten may I be!
Oh may no pitying thought of me
Disturb the joy that she may find,
When love is crown'd and fortune kind:
May that bless'd swain (whom yet I hate)
Be proud of his distinguish'd fate:
Each happy night be like the first;
And he be bless'd as I am curs'd.
Hoh, ho, ho, &c.

While in these pathless woods I stray,
And lose my solitary way;
Talk to the stars, to trees complain,
And tell the senseless words my pain:
But madness spares the sacred name,
Nor dares the hidden wound proclaim;
Which, secret rankling, sure and slow,
Shall close in endless peace my woe.
Hoh, ho, ho, &c.

When this fond heart shall ache no more,
And all the ills of life are o'er
(If gods by lovers' prayers are mov'd,
As ev'ry god in heaven has lov'd);
Instead of bright Elysian joys,
That unknown something in the skies,
In recompense of all my pain,
The only heaven I'd obtain,
May I, the guardian of her charms,
Preserve that paradise from harms.
Hoh, ho, ho, &c.

A HYMN TO THE MOON

Written in July, in an arbour

Thou silver deity of secret night,
Direct my footsteps through the woodland shade;
Thou conscious witness of unknown delight,
The Lover's guardian, and the Muse's aid!

By thy pale beams I solitary rove,
To thee my tender grief confide;
Serenely sweet you gild the silent grove,
My friend, my goddess, and my guide.

E'en thee, fair queen, from thy amazing height,
The charms of young Endymion drew;
Veil'd with the mantle of concealing night;
With all thy greatness and thy coldness too.

TRANSLATED BY HERSELF

Della notte serena argentea Diva,
Testimon' fido de' piaceri ignoti:
Custode degli amanti e delle Muse
Fautrice, reggi me ne'boschi oscuri.
Da' toui pallidi rai scorto io camino
Su la terra, ed a te svelo i piu cupi
Pensieri. Ah indora il tacitorno bosco,
Dolcemente serena amica mia,
E mia guida, e mia Dea. Bella reina,
Te dalla tua prodigiosa altezza
Il lusinghiero Endimione attrasse,
Del velo ingombra della notte oscura,
Della tua ampiezza in onta e del tuo gelo.

THE BRIDE IN THE COUNTRY

A Parody on Rowe's Ballad, "Despairing beside a clear stream," &c.

By the side of a half-rotten wood
Melantha sat silently down,
Convinc'd that her scheme was not good,
And vex'd to be absent from Town.
Whilst pitied by no living soul,
To herself she was forc'd to reply,
And the sparrow, as grave as an owl,
Sat list'ning and pecking hard by.

"Alas! silly maid that I was!"
Thus sadly complaining, she cried;
"When first I forsook that dear place,
'T had been better by far I had died!
How gaily I pass'd the long days,
In a round of continual delights;
Park, visits, assemblies, and plays,
And a dance to enliven the nights.

"How simple was I to believe

Delusive poetical dreams!
Or the flattering landscapes they give
Of meadows and murmuring streams.
Bleak mountains, and cold starving rocks,
Are the wretched result of my pains;
The swains greater brutes than their flocks,
The nymphs as polite as the swains.

"What though I have got my dear Phil;
I see him all night and all day;
I find I must not have my will,
And I've cursedly sworn to obey!
Fond damsel, thy power is lost,
As now I experience too late!
Whatever a lover may boast,
A husband is what one may hate!

"And thou, my old woman, so dear,
My all that is left of relief,
Whatever I suffer, forbear—
Forbear to dissuade me from grief:
'Tis in vain, as you say, to repine
At ills which cannot be redress'd;
But, in sorrows so poignant as mine,
To be patient, alas! is a jest.

"If, further to soothe my distress,
Your tender compassion is led,
Come hither and help to undress,
And decently put me to bed.
The last humble solace I wait,
Would Heav'n but indulge me the boon,
May some dream, less unkind than my fate,
In a vision transport me to Town.

"Clarissa, meantime, weds a beau,
Who decks her in golden array:
She's the finest at ev'ry fine show,
And flaunts it at Park and at Play:
Whilst I am here left in the lurch,
Forgot and secluded from view;
Unless when some bumpkin at church
Stares wistfully over the pew."

The following is another version of the preceding poem, as it was set to music, and called

MELINDA'S COMPLAINT

By the side of a glimmering fire,
Melinda sat pensively down,
Impatient of rural esquire,
And vex'd to be absent from Town.
The cricket, from under the grate,
With a chirp to her sighs did reply,
And the kitten, as grave as a cat,
Sat mournfully purring hard by.
"Alas! silly maid that I was!"
Thus sadly complaining, she cried;
"When first I forsook that dear place,
'T were better by far I had died!
How gaily I pass'd the long day,
In a round of continu'd delight;
Park, visits, assemblies, and play,
And quadrille to enliven the night.

"How simple was I to believe
Delusive poetical dreams!
The flattering landskips they give
Of groves, meads, and murmuring streams.
Bleak mountains, and wild staring rocks,
Are the wretched result of my pains;
The swains greater brutes than their flocks,
And the nymphs as polite as the swains.

"What though I have skill to ensnare,
Where Smarts in bright circles abound;
What though at St. James's at prayers,
Beaux ogle devoutly around:
Fond virgin, thy power is lost,
On a race of rude Hottentot brutes;
What glory in being the toast
Of noisy dull 'squires in boots?

"And thou, my companion, so dear,
My all that is left of relief,
Whatever I suffer, forbear—
Forbear to dissuade me from grief:
'Tis in vain then, you'll say to repine
At ills which cannot be redress'd,
But in sorrows so pungent as mine,
To be patient, alas! is a test.

"If, further to soothe my distress,
Thy tender compassion is led,

Call Jenny to help me undress,
And decently put me to bed.
The last humble solace I wait,
Would Heaven indulge me the boon,
Some dream less unkind than my fate,
In a vision transport me to Town.

"Clarissa, meantime, weds a beau,
Who decks her in golden array;
The finest at every fine show,
And flaunts it at Park and at Play;
Whilst here we are left in the lurch,
Forgot and secluded from view;
Unless when some bumpkin at church
Stares wistfully over the pew."

SONG

Why should you think I live unpleas'd,
Because I am not pleas'd with you?
My mind is not so far diseas'd,
To yield when powder'd fops pursue.

My vanity can find no charm
In common prostituted vows;
Nor can you raise a wish that's warm
In one that your true value knows.

While cold and careless thus I shun
The buzz and flutter that you make,
Perhaps some giddy girl may run
To catch the prize that I forsake.

So brightly shines the glittering glare,
In unexperienc'd children's eyes,
When they with little arts ensnare
The gaudy painted butterflies.

While they with pride the conquest boast,
And think the chase deserving care,
Those scorn the useless toil they cost
Who're us'd to more substantial fare.

SONG—RONDEAU

Finish these langours! Oh! I'm sick
Of dying airs, I know the trick;
Long since I've learn'd to well explain
Th'unmeaning cant of fire and pain,
And see through all the senseless lies
Of burning darts from killing eyes;
I'm tir'd with this continual rout
Of bowing low and leading out.
Finish, &c.

Finish this tedious dangling trade,
By which so many fools are made;
For fools they are, whom you can please
By such affected airs as these:
At opera near my box to stand,
And slyly press the given hand,
Thus may you wait whole years in vain;
But sure you would, were you in pain.
Finish, &c.

EPITHALAMIUM

Since you, Mr. H—d, will marry black Kate,
Accept of good wishes for that blessed state:
May you fight all the day like a dog and a cat,
And yet ev'ry year produce a new brat.
Fal la!

May she never be honest—you never be sound;
May her tongue like a clapper be heard a mile round;
Till abandon'd by joy, and deserted by grace,
You hang yourselves both in the very same place.
Fal la!

THE NINTH ODE OF THE THIRD BOOK OF HORACE IMITATED. 1736

"Donec gratus eram tibi."

SIR ROBERT WALPOLE
Whilst in each of my schemes you most heartily join'd,
And help'd the worst jobs that I ever design'd,
In pamphlets, in ballads, in senate, at table,
Thy satire was witty, thy counsel was able.

WILLIAM PULTENEY

Whilst with me you divided both profit and care,
And the plunder and glory did equally share;
Assur'd of his place, if my fat friend should die,
The Prince of Wales was not so happy as I.

SIR ROBERT WALPOLE

Harry Pelham{125} is now my support and delight,
Whom we bubble all day, and we joke on at night;
His head is well furnish'd, his lungs have their merit,
I would venture a rope to advance such a spirit.

WILLIAM PULTENEY

I too have a Harry more useful than yours,
Writes verses like mad, and will talk you whole hours;
I would bleed by the hatchet, or swing by the cord,
To see him once more in his robes, like a lord.

SIR ROBERT WALPOLE

But what if this quarrel was kindly made up?
Would you, my dear Willy, accept of a sup?
If the queen should confess, you had long been her choice,
And you knew it was I who had spoke in her voice?

WILLIAM PULTENEY

Though my Harry's so gay, so polite, and so civil,
You rude as a bear, and more proud than the devil,
I gladly would drop him, and laugh in your ear
At the fools we have made for this last dozen year.

A SUMMARY (*of Lord Lyttleton's advice to a Lady*)

"The counsels of a friend, Belinda, hear," &c.

Be plain in dress, and sober in your diet,
In short, my deary, kiss me! and be quiet.

SONG

Why will Delia thus retire,
And languish life away?
Why the sighing crows admire,
'Tis too soon for hartshorn tea.

All these dismal looks and fretting
Cannot Damon's life restore;
Long ago the worms have eat him,
You can never see him more.

Once again consult your toilet,
In the glass your face review;
So much weeping sure will spoil it,
And no springs your charms renew.

I, like you, was born a woman,
Well I know what vapours mean!
The disease, alas! is common,
Single we have all the spleen.

All the morals that they teach us
Never cur'd our sorrows yet:
Choose among the pretty fellows
One of humour, youth, and wit.

Prithee hear him ev'ry morning,
At the least an hour or two;
Once again at night returning,
I believe the dose will do.

THE SAME

translated by Lady M. W. Montagu.

Recipe per l'Eccelentissima Signora Chiara Michelli.

Vi consigliate con lo speccio, e il vostro
Viso mirate—lagrime cotante
Lo guasteranno, ed i perduti vezzi
Non avranno altra primavera. Io nacqui,
Donna, qual voi, e so qual voi la forza
Che hanno i vapori e infermita commune:
Tutte abbiam mal di milza, e non sanaro
Delle moral le massime piu saggi
Gli minimi neppur de'nostri guai.
Il piu amabile voi tra tanti amanti
Sceglier vi piaccia, e sopra tutto quello
Chi piu degli altri ha gioventude e spirito;
Io vi prego d'udirlo un ora al giorno,
Ed un altra la sera, e questo dose

Sia bastante rimedio al vostro male.

THE POLITICIANS

In ancient days when every brute
To humble privilege had right;
Could reason, wrangle, or dispute,
As well as scratch, and tear, and bite;

When Phoebus shone his brightest ray,
The rip'ning corn his pow'r confessed;
His cheering beams made Nature gay,
The eagle in his warmth was blest.

But malcontents e'en then arose,
The birds who love the dolesome night
The darkest grove with care they chose,
And there caball'd against the light.

The screech-owl, with ill-boding cry,
Portends strange things, old women say,
Stops ev'ry fool that passes by,
And frights the schoolboy from his play.

The raven and the double bat,
With families of owls combine;
In close consult they rail and chat,
And curse aloud the glorious shine.

While the great planet, all serene,
Heedless pursues his destin'd way,
He asks not what these murmurs mean,
But runs his course, and gives us day.

BALLAD, ON A LATE OCCURRENCE

Ungodly papers ev'ry week
Poor simple souls persuade
That courtiers good for nothing are,
Or but for mischief made.

But I who know their worthy hearts,
Pronounce that we are blind,
Who disappoint their honest schemes,

Who would be just and kind.

For in this vile degen'rate age
'Tis dangerous to do good;
Which will, when I have told my tale,
Be better understood.

A puppy, gamesome, blithe, and young,
Who play'd about the court,
Was destin'd by unlucky boys,
To be their noonday's sport.

With flatt'ring words they him entic'd,
(Words such as much prevail!)
And then with cruel art they tied
A bottle to his tail.

Lord Hervey at a window stood,
Detesting of the fact;
And cried aloud with all his might,
"I know the bottle's crack'd.

"Do not to such a dirty hole
Let them your tail apply;
Alas! you cannot know these things
One half so well as I.

"Harmless and young, you don't suspect
The venom of this deed;
But I see through the whole design,—
It is to make you bleed."

This good advice was cast away;
The puppy saw it shine;
And tamely lick'd their treach'rous hands,
And thought himself grown fine.

But long he had not worn the gem,
But as Lord Hervey said,
He ran and bled; the more he ran,
Alas! the more he bled.

Griev'd to the soul, this gallant lord
Tripp'd hastily down stairs;
With courage and compassion fir'd,
To set him free prepares.

But such was his ingratitude

To this most noble lord,
He bit his lily hand quite through,
As he untied the cord.

Next day the Maids of Honour came,
As I heard people tell;
They wash'd the wound with brinish tears,
—And yet it is not well.

Oh! gen'rous youth, my counsel take,
And warlike acts forbear;
Put on white gloves, and lead folks out,
—For that is your affair.

Never attempt to take away
Bottles from others' tails,
For that is what no soul will bear
From Italy to Wales.

SONG

Blame not that love, too cruel fair,
Which your own charms did first create;
Blame not my silence and despair,—
Such crimes can ne'er deserve your hate:
Why should your eyes first stir desire?
Your matchless wit, why fan the fire?
Repentance comes too late.
Vain are the vows that you complain
Are to another fondly made;
All your advice to me's as vain;
You must not—cannot be obey'd;
My heart can't change, though you command,
Nor can my heart obey your hand!
Love's power none can evade!

VERSES, WRITTEN IN A GARDEN

See how the pair of billing doves
With open murmurs own their loves;
And, heedless of censorious eyes,
Pursue their unpolluted joys;
No fears of future want molest
The downy quiet of their nest:

No int'rest join'd the happy pair,
Securely blest in Nature's care,
While her dictates they pursue;
For constancy is Nature too.
Can all the doctrine of the schools,
Our maxims, our religious rules,
Can learning to our lives ensure,
Virtue so bright, or bliss so pure?
The great Creator's happy ends
Virtue and pleasure ever blends:
In vain the Church and Court have tried
Th'united essence to divide;
Alike they find their wild mistake,
The pedant priest and giddy rake.

SONG

Fond wishes you pursue in vain,
My heart is vow'd away and gone;
Forbear thy sighs, too, lovely swain,
Those dying airs that you put on!
Go try on other maids your art,
Ah! leave this lost unworthy heart,
But you must leave it soon.
Such sighs as these you should bestow
On some unpractis'd blooming fair;
Where rosy youth doth warmly glow,
Whose eyes forbid you to despair.
Not all thy wond'rous charms can move
A heart that must refuse your love,
Or not deserve your care.

IMPROMPTU, TO A YOUNG LADY SINGING.

Sing, gentle maid—reform my breast,
And soften all my care;
Thus may I be some moments blest,
And easy in despair.
The pow'r of Orpheus lives in you;
You can the passions of my soul subdue,
And tame the lions and the tigers there.

ADVICE

Cease, fond shepherd—cease desiring
What you never must enjoy;
She derides your vain aspiring,
She to all your sex is coy.

Cunning Damon once pursu'd her,
Yet she never would incline;
Strephon too as vainly woo'd her,
Though his flocks are more than thine.

At Diana's shrine aloud,
By the zone around her waist,
Thrice she bow'd, and thrice she vow'd
Like the Goddess to be chaste.

ANSWER

Though I never got possession,
'Tis a pleasure to adore;
Hope, the wretch's only blessing,
May in time procure me more.

Constant courtship may obtain her,—
Where both wealth and merit fail,
And the lucky minute gain her,—
Fate and fancy must prevail.

At Diana's shrine aloud,
By the bow and by the quiver,
Thrice she bow'd, and thrice she vow'd,
Once to love—and that forever.

EPISTLE TO LORD HERVEY ON THE KING'S BIRTHDAY. FROM THE COUNTRY.

Where I enjoy in contemplative chamber,
Lutes, laurels, seas of milk, and ships of amber.

Through shining crowds you now make way,
With sideling bow and golden key;
While wrapped in spleen and easy-chair,
For all this pomp so small my care,
I scarce remember who are there.

Yet in brocade I can suppose
The potent Knight whose presence goes
At least a yard before his nose:
And majesty with sweeping train,
That does so many yards contain,
Superior to her waiting nymphs,
As lobster to attendant shrimps.
I do not ask one word of news,
Which country damsels much amuse.
If a new batch of Lords appears,
After a tour of half six years,
With foreign years to grace the nation,
The Maids of Honour's admiration;
Whose bright improvements give surprise
To their own lady-mother's eyes:
Improvements, such as colts might show,
Were mares so mad to let them go;
Their limbs perhaps a little stronger,
Their manes and tails grown somewhat longer.
I would not hear of ball-room scuffles,
Nor what new whims adorn the ruffles.
This meek epistle comes to tell,
On Monday, I in town shall dwell;
Where, if you please to condescend
In Cavendish-square to see your friend,
I shall disclose to you alone
Such thoughts as ne'er were thought upon.

EPIGRAM, 1734

Born to be slaves, our fathers freedom sought,
And with their blood the precious treasure bought;
We their mean offspring our own bondage plot,
And, born to freedom, for our chains we vote.

AN ANSWER TO A LADY

Who Advised Lady M. W. Montagu to Retire.

You little know the heart that you advise:
I view this various scene with equal eyes;
In crowded courts I find myself alone,
And pay my worship to a nobler throne.

Long since the value of this world I know;
Pitied the folly, and despis'd the show;
Well as I can, my tedious part I bear,
And wait dismissal without pain or fear.

Seldom I mark mankind's detested ways,
Not hearing censure or affecting praise;
And unconcern'd my future fate I trust
To that sole Being, merciful and just!

WRITTEN AT LOVERE, OCTOBER, 1736

If age and sickness, poverty and pain,
Should each assault me with alternate plagues,
I know mankind is destin'd to complain,
And I submit to torment and fatigues.
The pious farmer, who ne'er misses pray'rs,
With patience suffers unexpected rain;
He blesses Heav'n for what its bounty spares,
And sees, resign'd, a crop of blighted grain.
But, spite of sermons, farmers would blaspheme,
If a star fell to set their thatch on flame.

CONCLUSION OF A LETTER TO A FRIEND

Sent from Italy, 1741.

But happy you from the contagion free,
Who, through her veil, can human nature see;
Calm you reflect, amid the frantic scene,
On the low views of those mistaken men,
Who lose the short invaluable hour,
Through dirt-pursuing schemes of distant pow'r:
Whose best enjoyments never pay the chase,
But melt like snow within a warm embrace.
Believe me, friend, for such indeed are you,
Dear to my heart, and to my int'rest true;
Too much already have you thrown away,
Too long sustain'd the labor of the day;
Enjoy the remnant of declining light,
Nor wait for rest till overwhelm'd in night.
By present pleasure balance pain you've past,
Forget all systems, and indulge your taste.

TO THE SAME

Wherever Fortune points my destin'd way,
If my capricious stars ordain my stay
In gilded palace, or in rural scene,
While breath shall animate this frail machine,
My heart sincere, which never flatt'ry knew,
Shall consecrate its warmest wish to you.
A monarch compass'd by a suppliant crowd,
Prompt to obey, and in his praises loud,
Amongst those thousands who on smiles depend,
Perhaps has no disinterested friend.

WRITTEN AT LOVERE, 1755

Wisdom, slow product of laborious years,
The only fruit that life's cold winter bears;
Thy sacred seeds in vain in youth we lay,
By the fierce storm of passion torn away.
Should some remain in a rich gen'rous soil,
They long lie hid, and must be rais'd with toil;
Faintly they struggle with inclement skies,
No sooner born than the poor planter dies.

LINES WRITTEN IN A BLANK PAGE OF MILTON'S PARADISE LOST

This happy pair a certain bliss might prove,
Confin'd to constancy and mutual love:
Heaven to one object limited their vows,
The only safety faithless Nature knows.
God saw the wand'ring appetite would range,
And would have kept them from the pow'r to change;
But falsehood, soon as man increas'd, began;
Down through the race the swift contagion ran,
All ranks are tainted, all deceitful prove,
False in all shapes, but doubly false in love.
This makes the censure of the world more just,
That damns with shame the weakness of a trust!
Ere change began, our sex no scandal knew,
All nymphs were chaste as long as swains were true;
But now, tho' by the subtlest art betray'd,
We're so by custom and false maxims sway'd

That infamy still brands the injur'd maid.

ADDRESSED TO —, 1736

With toilsome steps I pass thro' life's dull road
(No pack-horse half so tired of his load);
And when this dirty journey will conclude,
To what new realms is then my way pursued?
Say, then does the unbodied spirit fly
To happier climes and to a better sky?
Or, sinking, mixes with its kindred clay,
And sleeps a whole eternity away?
Or shall this form be once again renew'd,
With all its frailties, all its hopes, endu'd;
Acting once more on this detested stage
Passions of youth, infirmities of age?
I see in Tully what the ancients thought,
And read unprejudic'd what moderns taught;
But no conviction from my reading springs—
Most dubious on the most important things.
Yet one short moment would at once explain
What all philosophy has sought in vain;
Would clear all doubt, and terminate all pain.
Why then not hasten that decisive hour;
Still in my view, and ever in my pow'r?
Why should I drag along this life I hate,
Without one thought to mitigate the weight?
Whence this mysterious bearing to exist,
When ev'ry joy is lost, and ev'ry hope dismiss'd?
In chains and darkness wherefore should I stay,
And mourn in prison whilst I keep the key?

18565214R00046